Mending

Broken Relationships,

Building

Strong Ones

Eight Ways to Love
as Jesus Loves Us

D1425149

Mending

Broken Relationships,

Building

Strong Ones

*Eight Ways to Love
as Jesus Loves Us*

John and Therese Boucher

the**WORD**
among us®
press

The Word Among Us Press
7115 Guilford Drive, Suite 100
Frederick, Maryland 21704
www.wau.org

19 18 17 16 15   1 2 3 4 5

ISBN: 978-1-59325-277-9
eISBN: 978-1-59325-470-4

Cover design by Andrea Alvarez

Made and printed in the United States of America

Library of Congress Control Number: 2015943531

To Bishop Timothy J. Harrington (1918–1997),
our first mentor in the art of loving the poor
in body, mind, and spirit.

Contents

INTRODUCTION

Ever met someone you just can't stand? We have. John had difficulties with a woman who struck him as distant, absorbed in her own circle of friends, and much too thin to be attractive. Therese was unimpressed by a young man who wore baggy work pants and was much too talkative and anxious to please. They had been thrown together as part of the same retreat team and then in the same inner-city group of parish volunteers. So the aggravation went on and on—until God finally stepped in and showed us the way.

If you haven't already guessed, John's nemesis was Therese. And Therese's source of irritation was John. As you can see, we are not experts on love—and we're still learning! But we know from experience that without God's intervention, it's impossible to mend relationships and build strong ones. And like so many saints before us, we also know that loving others requires following Jesus on the path of love. If you believe that too, and if you are tired of coping with less than fulfilling relationships and want to make some changes, then we are certain that God can help you.

What is the basis of our certainty? First, if you have been baptized, you were baptized into Trinitarian love—Father, Son, and Holy Spirit. Through Baptism, you became a fledgling apprentice in the art of receiving and reflecting God's love. And even now, the waters of God's life continuously wash over you, strengthening you and giving you all that you need to be a caring disciple of Jesus. You can be an instrument of God's love by following the path of your Teacher. And even though you may have made mistakes, the Holy Spirit is willing to help you start the Christian life all over again, every day or every hour if necessary. God's grace is there for you as you face the challenges of being your brother's keeper or your sister's friend in the Lord. God will help you learn how to love as you surrender to the ongoing transformation that our Father offers, especially through daily prayer.

Second, remember that Jesus has died for you—and for all of our relationships. He is risen and shares his resurrection and new life with us. And Christ sends his Holy Spirit to us, bringing healing between us. Christ knows our desolation. When we face the struggles and difficult emotions that plague every human relationship, we can choose Jesus as our companion. He will bring new life and healing to our relationships, as long as we surrender to his wisdom and follow him into our daily lives. He can transform our moments of desolation into times of joy and consolation.

Third, virtues like respect, forgiveness, gratitude, affirming others, forbearance, patience, honesty, and a healing presence are given to you as gifts through the power of the Holy Spirit. And like seeds that are planted in the earth, these virtues and gifts can grow with prayer, mutual support, and practice.

So take heart. You are empowered to build life-giving relationships that both imitate Christ's life and connect others to Jesus. And through your efforts to follow Jesus and your ongoing surrender to the Holy Spirit, you can create an atmosphere of love in which these virtues become tested paths for relationships and for building up the body of Christ. Through grace, you and those you love will be grafted, as small twigs or large branches, onto an ever-expanding vine that courses with the love of the Trinity in your daily life.

Pathways for Growing in Love

We suspect that you picked up this book for a reason. Maybe you feel incapable of love right now or are agonizing over a particular broken relationship. Here is the approach that we will use for each chapter as we explore ways to mend and strengthen relationships. Our hope is that you discover or rediscover Jesus, who is the source of love, the master architect for building and repairing personal relationships.

Each of the eight chapters is designed to be a pathway toward realizing God's love and connecting others to Jesus. And each pathway, while important in itself, is meant to merge with the other pathways we discuss. For example, there is a chapter on gratitude and another on affirmation. These two pathways often work together: it is when we are filled with gratitude for what someone has done for us that we are moved by God to thank and affirm that person.

As you pray along each path, you will be traveling "the way"— the broad highway to God's kingdom with your brothers and sisters in Christ. That "way" is Jesus. In fact, the Acts of the Apostles refers to all Christians as followers of "the Way" (9:2; 19:23), and Jesus himself says he is "the way, and the truth, and the life" (John 14:6).

So the most important first step in learning how to love is to turn to Jesus, our teacher, who shows us how to move beyond our failings. In the first section of each chapter, we will delve into the Scriptures and consider how Jesus forged each path to love. In the chapter on respect, for example, we will consider Jesus' meeting with the Samaritan woman at the well as an extraordinary example of respect. Jesus appreciated her in ways that no one else could.

In section two of each chapter, we'll consider ways in which we can surrender to God's love and gifts. There are so many ways to give love in our lives, but it's just as important to learn how to expand our capacity to receive love. So we will share the struggles involved in receiving and surrendering to gifts such as healing, patience, and forgiveness in the context of a vital daily relationship with God. After all, we can't give what we do not have.

In the third section of each chapter, we will present a "first aid kit" for the times when building a life of holiness and love seems to be impossible in your daily relationships with others. There will be examples from our own lives, helpful Scripture verses, and quotes from the lives of the saints, who are models of the Church's teaching about love. In particular, we will include quotes from Pope Francis about loving others, especially from his apostolic exhortation *The Joy of the Gospel*.

Each chapter will end with reflection questions and an exercise that you can use to grow as a caring missionary disciple of Jesus. And throughout the book, there will be stories from the lives of many people who have inspired us by the ways in which they strive to learn from Christ and to mend relationships instead of abandoning them.

So let us begin life's greatest and most satisfying adventure. Let us move beyond wallowing in our faltering ability to love. Let us surrender all of our broken relationships to God and begin again with a willingness to learn from Jesus. Let us move forward with the confidence and zeal of St. Thérèse of Lisieux (1873–1897), who exclaimed, "At last I have found my calling! My calling is love!"[1]

John and Therese Boucher

CHAPTER ONE

INTERCESSORY PRAYER

The buzzer sounded so loud and harsh that John could hear it through the thick wooden door to the rectory. "What am I doing here?" he thought to himself as he saw the face of the gruff old priest appear in the tiny side window. Not many in the parish would approach Fr. Wilfred's door unless some kind of important business required a visit. And John had no such business. But over the previous month or two, he had prayed for the parish often, and speaking with Fr. Wilfred seemed like a good first step toward finding a way to serve.

Over the next two years, John and Fr. Wilfred enjoyed many conversations about ministry in the parish. During some conversations, the priest listened as John spoke about his call to lay ministry. During other visits, John listened to Fr. Wilfred's concerns about his failing health or the problems in the parish. As the months went by, John realized that the most important thing he could do for this parish was to pray for Fr. Wilfred every day and to continue their visits. John's final visit was to Fr. Wilfred's wake. He was stunned by the greeting from another priest of the parish: "Thanks for coming. Fr. Wilfred thought of you as one of his best friends."

What moves you to pray and reach out to others? How do you pray for the difficult people and situations in your life? Do you complain? Do you plead for God's help in mending what is broken? Do you recognize God's invitation to love at the root of all your concerns? How often do you cross the threshold of prayer in order to grow in the depth of God's love for the people in your life?

Jesus and Intercessory Prayer

Mark's Gospel tells us that following Jesus' baptism, "the Spirit immediately drove him out into the wilderness. He was in the wilderness forty days, tempted by Satan; and he was with the wild beasts; and the angels waited on him" (1:12-13). For Jesus, prayer was the beginning of his ministry and the ongoing foundation for all that he did to reach out to others. Mark's story also reminds us that Jesus was no stranger to the struggles we face in prayer. Yet he persisted in seeking intimacy with the Father in prayer. He also drew strength from these honest conversations with the Father as he prayed for his disciples and for all of his followers.

The Scriptures also give us many glimpses of Jesus going beyond himself to intercede for others in prayer. Some of these examples illustrate the connection between intercessory prayer and healing. For example, Jesus took a deaf man aside, put his fingers in the man's ear, looked up to heaven in prayer, and then restored the man's hearing (Mark 7:31-35). On another occasion, Jesus went to the tomb of his friend Lazarus, where he thanked his Father for raising Lazarus even before it happened (John 11:41-44).

Still more examples show Jesus praying for his disciples when they misunderstand or fail him. Before Peter's denial of Jesus, Jesus told him, "I have prayed for you that your own faith may not fail; and you, when once you have turned back, strengthen your brothers" (Luke 22:32). And finally, near the end of his life on earth, Jesus prayed with intense concern and unending affection for all of his future followers: "Holy Father, protect them in your name that you have given me, so that they may be one, as we are one" (John 17:11).

Praying for others is such an enduring reality for Jesus that he is described in Scripture as sitting at the right hand of God, interceding for us (Romans 8:34). So even now, Jesus prays as "a great high priest" (Hebrews 4:14), offering the eternal sacrifice of prayer and praise. "Consequently he is able for all time to save those who approach God through him, since he always lives to make intercession for them" (7:25). This means that Jesus is already praying for you and beckoning you to join him in prayer for the people you encounter in your daily life. Will you spend time before Jesus? Will you accept this gift of prayer? Will you offer all the people in your life to God, even the troublesome ones? Will you choose to draw new strength to love and new graces for connecting others to Jesus?

Surrendering to the Gift of Intercessory Prayer

Perhaps you have already prayed for others and have experienced only frustration and disappointment. Perhaps you find yourself avoiding intercessory prayer because of the raw and painful emotions that surface. Paul encourages all of us to persevere in prayer beyond our spiritual and emotional poverty: "Likewise the Spirit helps us in our weakness; for we do not know how to pray as we ought, but that very Spirit intercedes with sighs too deep for words. And God, who searches the heart, knows what is the mind of the Spirit" (Romans 8:26-27).

Therese learned a lot about surrendering to the gift of intercessory prayer when she prayed for her new co-worker, Fr. Eddie. At the time, she didn't really know him very well, and she sensed a strain in their relationship, probably because the projects they had begun tackling together were demanding and innovative. Fr. Eddie was also undergoing treatment for early-stage lung cancer. A few days after a round of chemotherapy, he was rushed to the hospital with pneumonia. When Therese walked into the ICU, she was shocked. Fr. Eddie's face and hands were so swollen and distorted that he was unrecognizable. There was a maze of tubes and monitors, and a prolonged drug-induced coma made conversation impossible.

To make matters worse, Fr. Eddie was in a hospital hundreds of miles from his home and most of his friends. So Therese felt called to pray in Fr. Eddie's hospital room once or twice a week. First she would say hello to him, in case he could hear her. Then she would sit in a chair and pray for him. It was often a raw and troubling experience, but it was also an opportunity to delve into the depths of intercessory prayer. Therese sensed the Spirit interceding through sighs, through Hail Marys, through music and pleading, and through Scripture readings. Weeks and weeks went by, which included at least two medical complications that almost took his life.

Through e-mails and cards from mutual friends and encounters with Fr. Eddie's former colleagues who joined her in prayer at his bedside, Therese witnessed the body of Christ praying together. Finally, Fr. Eddie was slowly weaned from his tracheotomy tube and drug-induced coma and began to recover. It was then that Therese realized that she had gone from a casual relationship with a co-worker to accepting Fr. Eddie as a brother and friend in Jesus. Through this adversity and through prayer, their relationship had been strengthened. She could truly say with Paul,

> In all these things we are more than conquerors through him who loved us. For I am convinced that neither death, nor life, nor angels, nor rulers, nor things present, nor things to come, nor powers, nor height, nor depth, nor anything else in all creation, will be able to separate us from the love of God in Christ Jesus our Lord. (Romans 8:37-39)

The truth behind intercessory prayer is that we join in God's work to overcome all obstacles to his love for us and for others. We might use psalms, readings from daily Mass, visits to the Blessed Sacrament, silence, tears, our own descriptions of others' needs, or worship music. The possibilities are endless but the decision is the same. We submit ourselves and others to God in prayer because it is difficult to love and offer support without first bringing another before God. And by choosing prayer, we trust God to change our hearts and make us more capable of reflecting his love and connecting others to Jesus, who is "the way, and the truth, and the life" (John 14:6).

God's Invitation to Intercessory Prayer

Ever watch two small children who want the same toy and quickly resort to grabbing, crying, and a burst of accusations? Then a frustrated adult steps in with an unsuccessful "Be nice!" or "Share!" This strategy usually doesn't work. The two children need more than vague directions. And so do we! Too often we are just like those preschoolers. We need something more than commands and homilies about being "nice." We need ongoing, specific guidance. An important way to receive such help involves the kind of daily prayer that reshapes us and makes us more capable of loving and sharing. Here are some suggestions that you can use often as you bring your relationships to God in prayer.

First: Choose a Primary Relationship with Jesus through Prayer

When you approach Jesus as the most important person in your life, you resist "clock time." You step away from the parade of numbered moments that tempt you to forget God as the source of all time, all goodness, and all love. When you pray, you enter into the "fullness of time" (Galatins 4:4) and anticipate the presence of Jesus in the midst of all other relationships. Not to choose Jesus first is to live in a topsy-turvy world of fragmented, broken, and disappointing relationships, where love is a fleeting phenomenon. We pray because we are convinced that ignoring Jesus, who wants to be our best friend, Savior, and brother, is to make gods or demons of other people, especially our loved ones. St. Teresa of Avila (1515–1582) counseled her sisters this way: "I cannot understand why [those who serve God and desire to serve Him] abandon prayer, unless it is that they want to undergo the trials of life with greater trials and close the door on God so that He may not make them happy."[2]

Second: Choose God as the Source of All Love and Strength

God is the source of all that we are and have: "In him we live and move and have our being" (Acts 17:28). Furthermore, God is love itself. Coming back to God is like returning to a community well at the center of a village. No matter how large or small your "pitcher," through prayer God fills you and sustains you with living water. Then you are enabled to care for others in the village of faith.

Scripture urges us in many ways to rely on God for the strength to love. In John's Gospel, Jesus reveals that he is the vine and we are the branches, passing along nutrients to others in order to yield the fruit of God's abiding love (15:1-11). St. Paul exhorts us to recall that Jesus tells us, "My grace is sufficient for you, for power is made perfect in weakness" (2 Corinthians 12:9). And in the Beatitudes, Jesus invites us to be both poor in spirit and merciful (Matthew 5:3, 7). Through prayer you can admit your poverty and allow God to expose your failings and your short-comings. Then by grace you will receive the ability to look beyond your own capacity to love. St. Teresa of Avila reminds us, "Souls without prayer are like people whose bodies or limbs are para-lyzed: they possess feet and hands but they cannot control them. But souls of prayer rejoice in saying, 'I can do all things in him who strengthens me' (Philippians 4:13)."[3]

Third: Use Difficulties, Emotions, and Brokenness as Doorways to Prayer

St. Gregory the Great (540–604) wrote, "In the shipwreck of this present life, sustain me by the plank of prayer, lest I sink by my own weight. Instead, let the hand of your mercy raise me up."[4] We watched our daughter Rose experience one of life's shipwrecks at the end of her first semester in college. A letter followed her home, stating that her decision to skip a lengthy final paper would mean a failing grade and the loss of a substantial scholarship. She would have to leave school. All three of us were in shock. No one had to remind us to pray, but how? All of our raw feelings tumbled out at the feet of Jesus.

Then we disciplined ourselves by giving Rose back to God, surrendering to him her college career and her future. That gave us enough peace to speak with her about her options. Then Rose called the head of her theater and costuming department for his advice. More prayer followed while she was on the phone. After listening, Dr. Morton decided to help her by restructuring her credits. He gave her credits for extra work that she had done in the studio and reclassified the course in question. All was forgiven. God had truly raised her up, given her back her scholarship, and honored our prayers of surrender.

Prayers of petition are meant to be a first small step in pursuing God's presence amidst difficulties. Too often we get stuck when something bad happens and rush to conclude that God isn't listening. Instead, we must imitate Jesus: "Let the same mind be in you that was in Christ Jesus, / who, though he was in the form of God, / . . . emptied himself, / taking the form of a slave"

(Philippians 2:5-7). Simply lay all of your needs before God; then empty yourself of expectations and demands. It is in surrendering all things to God that we are truly able to grow in prayer and in love for others.

Fourth: Consecrate Another to God

If a surgeon were operating on your loved one, would you allow yourself to be so overcome that you would rush in and take the scalpel out of his hand? No. You would stand outside the door and pray. You would ask Jesus to go into the operating room in your place. You would ask God to guide the surgeon's hands, mind, and heart.

And so it is with intercessory prayer. There is a moment when you step back and wait, but it's not a fretful kind of waiting. You wait for Jesus—the surgeon, healer, and redeemer. And while you are waiting, you make the sacrifice of consecrating this person to God: "I do not own him. I have no claims on her when we both stand before you, Father." To sacrifice literally means to "make holy." And it is in surrendering another to God that we become holy in one another's eyes. Our eyes are opened to see what God might do next in our relationships as well.

Therese's sister Susan had faithfully cared for their father for many years. After Dad's death and the impending sale of the family house, Susan needed housing—and quickly—because the new owner's arrival was just a few weeks away. Everyone was deeply concerned because Susan was at the bottom of a city-housing placement list. So during a family get-together, Susan, Therese, and their cousin Carol huddled together in prayer. They began by thanking

God for all the caregiving that Susan had done. Then they surrendered her and her situation to Jesus. Therese was inspired to pray, "And please give her an apartment by Easter, Lord." And that is exactly what happened. Susan moved into her first-choice building just a month later and a few days before Palm Sunday.

Here is what Pope Francis wrote about intercessory prayer in his apostolic exhortation *The Joy of the Gospel*:

> [Intercessory prayer] is a spiritual gaze born of deep faith which acknowledges what God is doing in the lives of others. At the same time, it is the gratitude which flows from a heart attentive to others. When evangelizers rise from prayer, their hearts are more open; freed of self-absorption, they are desirous of doing good and sharing their lives with others. The great men and women of God were great intercessors. Intercession is like a "leaven" in the heart of the Trinity. It is a way of penetrating the Father's heart and discovering new dimensions which can shed light on concrete situations and change them.[5]

Fifth: Pray for the Gifts and Fruits of the Holy Spirit

When you were baptized and confirmed, you were given the gifts and fruits of the Holy Spirit, enabling you to love like Jesus. God wants to increase these gifts in you, along with a hunger for greater holiness in your relationships with those in your daily life. This same desire for holiness, for love, and for the fruits of the Spirit can be seen in the lives of many saints. So reading about the saints can help you discover new ways the Spirit might work in your relationships. Learning about the exercise of these gifts can also help you develop inner images for sacrificial, holy love. Start by studying the saint of the day until you find one that inspires you. Then delve more deeply into that particular saint's relationship with God and others.

Reading Scripture can also encourage you to seek God's gifts for the sake of others. As you pray with various passages, the Holy Spirit will encourage you to focus on a particular gift or fruit of the Spirit.[6] John spent a number of months asking God for the gifts of wisdom and discernment, especially so that he could recognize someone who is searching for God. Then he tried listening for the weight of God's voice behind needs that others described to him. For example, during a visit to some relatives, we excused ourselves to go to Mass. While there, he prayed for our hostess, who had made a remark about struggling with fatigue. When we returned to her home, she asked, "Did you pray for me?" and John was able to say, "Yes, I did!"

Therese often prays for the gift of a healing presence, whether this means listening with compassion or surrendering someone to God through intercessory prayer. One night several years ago, she woke up in the middle of a nightmare about a friend named Jim. In the dream, they were at a church gathering, and Jim's neck fell to one side like a broken rag doll. Then he screamed out in pain, and she ran over to hold up his head. The dream was so real that Therese got up and prayed for Jim for about an hour and then went back to sleep. To her amazement, the next day she found out that Jim had been in a car accident and had broken his neck. His car had flipped over, and while he dangled upside down, he heard a voice saying, "Don't move your head. Don't move your head." So he didn't. And even though his neck was broken, there was no lasting damage. What a privilege it was for Therese to be a part of God's healing mercy! What a blessing for all of us to serve God through prayer and beyond!

Pope St. John Paul II (1920–2005) wrote,

> Being a follower of Christ means *becoming conformed to him* who became a servant even to giving himself on the Cross (cf. Philippians 2:5-8). Christ dwells by faith in the heart of the believer (cf. Ephesians 3:17), and thus the disciple is conformed to the Lord. This is the *effect of grace*, of the active presence of the Holy Spirit in us.[7]

Sixth: Join Your Prayers to the Prayers of the Church

If you have ever prayed for someone for a long time, you can relate to Moses' experience as he prayed for the Israelites as they battled the Amalekites: "But Moses' [upstretched] hands grew weary; so . . . Aaron and Hur held up his hands, one on one side, and the other on the other side; so his hands were steady until the sun set" (Exodus 17:12). And the battle was won! Intercessory prayer is a gift that is given to the whole body of Christ, and each of us will experience more peace as we join our prayers with the prayers of others. This can be done in many ways: praying with a friend for each other's concerns, praying the Rosary for specific intentions, or bringing your prayer intentions to Mass by reading your list (privately) after the prayers of the faithful. You might also pray an Our Father or Hail Mary right on the spot when someone asks you for prayer.

In the early nineties, people in our part of the country were excited about a rare opportunity to see a space shuttle fly by. That morning Therese scurried off toward a field where a dozen eager people were watching the sky. But she had misjudged the distance and didn't arrive in time to see the shuttle. What Therese did see was just as impressive. The sighting of the shuttle had moved the twelve spectators in a dramatic way. Some jumped. Some pointed. Some waved and shouted, "Hello!" All of them cheered in unison and began to chatter about what they had seen. This experience gave Therese a visual image for looking toward Jesus together in prayer. Jesus moves us in unison, Jesus empowers us to see, and then Jesus sets us on fire to share and to love in our everyday world. As Pope Benedict wrote, "I cannot possess Christ just for myself; I can belong to him only in union with all those who have become, or who will become, his own."[8]

Questions for Reflection

1. How much of your prayer time is spent in praying for others, as opposed to worshipping God, reading Scripture, or other devotional practices? What is it like for you to pray for others? What effect does this prayer have on your relationships with others?

2. What would it be like to pray for the difficult people in your life? What does it mean to consecrate them to God? How has God helped you move beyond difficulties as you pray for them?

3. What helps you understand God's loving compassion for others? How could you imitate the compassion of Jesus more often in your relationships? What obstacles to love might you surrender to God?

4. What is one insight you have gained from this chapter? How could you put it into practice in your daily life?

Skills for Growing through Intercessory Prayer

Imagine yourself at the first Pentecost, when the Holy Spirit came down on the frightened and confused disciples of Jesus (Acts 2). Ask God to make you capable of sharing your faith, especially by connecting others to Jesus in prayer. Then reach out to God using the names and titles for the Holy Spirit that come from Scripture and Church teaching.

Step One: *Choose at least one or two titles that touch you. Repeat them over and over again slowly.*

Advocate • Comforter • Gift of God • Breath of God
Counselor • Teacher • Power of the Most High
Soul of the Church • Breath of Heaven • Helper
Living Flame of Love • Spirit of Jesus • Paraclete
Giver of Gifts • Holy Ghost • Consoler • Divine Light
Giver of Life • Spirit of Truth • Wisdom • Sanctifier
Spirit of Understanding • Great Evangelizer
Strength of God • Guardian

Step Two: *Slow down your breathing so that your body can become more involved in prayer. Intersperse the titles that touch you with your requests to love specific people in your life. You can repeat each prayer as needed.*

Step Three: *Pray the following, using both the names for the Spirit and the name of the person for whom you wish to pray:*

Come Holy Spirit, Come (insert one title). Fill my heart. Help me love (name).

Come Holy Spirit, Come (insert title). Transform the way I listen to (name).

Come Holy Spirit, Come (insert title). Use me to bless my loved ones and all the people in my daily life, especially (name).

I ask all this in the name of the Father, and of the Son, and of the Holy Spirit. Amen.

CHAPTER TWO

RESPECT

It was a hot and dusty summer. We were part of a team of college students who had volunteered to visit the parishioners of St. John's. As we approached the inner-city neighborhood, we felt like pioneers. Even though it was just a few miles from where we lived, it was isolated, hemmed in by freeway ramps and several abandoned factories, and suffering from rampant poverty.

The work was challenging, but John was delighted when he was able to help one woman return to the sacraments after several decades of being away. However, the greatest challenge we faced as leaders of the team had nothing to do with the people we visited. Our constant struggle was in being Christlike and respectful toward one another on the team. Some were always late. Some had conflicting approaches to visiting and to offering parish services. There were noticeable tensions.

The tension came to a climax one night when one of the volunteers on our team, Jason, got drunk during an open house. As the leaders of the group, we were angry, and Jason knew it! So he staggered out the door and tumbled down a narrow, winding flight of stairs. His injures warranted a speeding ambulance ride and an all-night vigil in the ER waiting room. Sometime around six the next morning, we were informed that Jason was going to be okay; God had protected him. And because of Jason's accident, the whole team had the grace to see past annoyances and grow in the gifts of kindness and respect.

When have you been challenged to respect someone? The word "respect," from the Latin *respectus*, literally means the "act of looking back (or often) at someone." We all know how difficult it can be to give up first impressions, rumors, and half-truths. When have you chosen God's vision as a yardstick for a first or second look at another person, with an eye toward their inner goodness? Let's reexamine God's invitation to see others with new eyes as Jesus did.

Jesus and Respect

Jesus had a tremendous capacity for seeing others in new ways. He did not look at sinners in the same way others did. According to the religious leaders around him, he was blind to who was clean or unclean, who was touchable or untouchable. Jesus ate with sinners! He touched lepers! He spoke with a Samaritan woman! He paid attention to annoying children! He welcomed tax collectors, notorious for their practice of extortion.

Was he blind? Of course not! Jesus saw every person through the lens of his Father's love. He loved everyone who approached him for help. His response to the rich young man was to look on him with love (Mark 10:21). And his revolutionary way of seeing others went beyond just the individual person. We find him weeping for a whole city (Luke 19:41-42). This episode—and indeed his whole ministry—is marked by a longing for God's people to open their eyes and recognize the peace and wholeness being offered to them.

Jesus saw the goodness and potential of many individuals in the Gospels. One striking example occurred in his relationship with

Peter. As mentioned earlier, Jesus prayed for Peter to be strong during Jesus' arrest, crucifixion, and death. To ordinary eyes, these prayers "did not work." When a servant girl challenged Peter about his friendship with Jesus, Peter denied knowing him (Luke 22:54-62). How many of us can recall a similar incident, when someone has done exactly what we told them not to do? How many of us find it hard to forget such an offense and trust again? Not Jesus! Even after Peter's denial, Jesus trusted and respected Peter enough to single him out for a special ministry. "Feed my lambs . . . Tend my sheep . . . Feed my sheep" (John 21:15, 16, 17). Jesus invited Peter to walk on the waters of humility and confidence in his calling.

Just like Jesus, the early Christians in the Acts of the Apostles were challenged to see others with new eyes. The disciple Ananias objected to seeking out Paul, a known persecutor of Christians. God addressed his fears with these words: "Go, for he is an instrument whom I have chosen to bring my name before Gentiles" (Acts 9:15). So Ananias surrendered to God's vision of Paul. All the disciples were challenged to a new respect for each other during the Council of Jerusalem (15:1-15). Another example involved Peter's vision of "profane or unclean" animals that he was instructed to eat (10:14). While he was still puzzled about what he had seen, he was invited to the home of a Roman centurion named Cornelius, where God's invitation to respect Gentiles became apparent. Peter said, "I truly understand that God shows no partiality, but in every nation anyone who fears him and does what is right is acceptable to him. . . . He is Lord of all" (10:34-36).

Surrendering to the Gift of Self-Respect

In order to grow in respect for others, we must first respect ourselves. Spiritual author and Anglican priest Morton Kelsey wrote, "Deep in the heart of every man [or woman] is the fear that no one can abide him. This is the result of our separation from God, and only as the human soul is watered with concern and love can this disfigurement within be cleansed away and replaced by a new growth of security and self-respect."[9]

When Therese's dad died, she was tempted to think like an orphan and feel unloved. "The person who loved me most is no more," she thought." He stayed twenty-eight years longer than Mom did, but now that doesn't matter. He's gone too." God needed to restore and heal her of self-esteem issues tied up with her childhood. Her challenge was to find a way to place her pain before Jesus so that she could see her dad and her own life in a new light.

Part of God's solution was a decision on Therese's part to "take another look" at herself and her life. She sorted and scanned several hundred family photos so that all five of her siblings could enjoy them. It took months and more than a few tears, but the smiling faces that emerged on her computer screen, alongside the hymns she played, began to speak to her of God's enduring goodness. Picnics, Christmas gifts, trips to the zoo, graduations—all became evidence of God's love through her parents. This "second look" at her family was just what she needed.

Therese's "orphan-sized" hole is an example of our wounded human condition. Each of us is tempted to think that we are unloved. "What's the use of turning to Jesus?" we might think.

"He is just like everybody else who has rejected me." When this happens, call out to Jesus, your Shepherd, who promises to "restore your soul" (cf. Psalm 23:3). Accept his vision of who you are. Let him look at you with love and appreciation for who you are in your deepest self. Then you will be healed and given the gift of self-respect. Then loving your neighbor as you love yourself will be a good thing, not an exercise in selfishness that fails to connect others with God's love.

God's Invitation to Respect Others

When we went to cousin Albert's wake recently, we ran into a friend named Tom. During our conversation about Albert, Tom explained that he had come to "pay his respects." This is not a common saying any longer, but it rang true for us. We, too, had come to acknowledge Albert's unique goodness, evident throughout his whole life. Let's use this saying as a starting point for considering the ways in which we can take the long view and "pay our respects" to one another in daily life.

First: We Are Made in the Image of Our God

When we approach one another, each one of us is drawing near to a person created in the image and likeness of God. This is the deepest reality of every human person, as stated in Genesis 1:27. But as we continue reading the Book of Genesis, we learn about the fall of the whole human race and about our individual and communal tendency toward doing evil. In other words, we are made of precious metal, but we are tarnished. And unfortunately, it is the tendency toward evil that some of us latch onto as the most important reality about each other, even to the point of defining some people as our enemies. Jesus warned us against this behavior: "Love your enemies, do good to those who hate you, bless those who curse you, pray for those who abuse you" (Luke 6:27-28). These are hard words! We suspect that, just like us, most of you find such warnings to be very difficult to put into practice!

So what are we saying? The point is that we are all lacking in exercising the gift of respect, whether it is the capacity to recognize and respect God's image in each other or in ourselves. So ask Jesus for a new sensitivity to the Father's handiwork in the faces of those in your daily life. Ask for a new appreciation for the people God places in your path. Ask for the grace to take a second look. Then you will have a firm foundation for good relationships. And if you dare, ask the Holy Spirit to show you the reflection of God's face in those you think of as your enemies.

Retreat master and spiritual director Fr. Thomas Dubay has written about the profound effects of respecting others: "Just as the Father has loved all things into being and continues to love them into their continuing existence, so too the Christian is to love his brother [and sister] into existence. Our love not only responds to existing goodness. It is a gratuitous kind of love, . . . a being-bestowing love."[10] This is a refreshing and hopeful idea. When you acknowledge God's presence in the depths of someone's heart, you are participating in God's creative love for that person. You are giving a gift of wholeness. You are re-creating. You are connecting another to God rather than disconnecting him or her from the source of all happiness and peace.

Second: We Are All Family through Our Brother Jesus

One time John's job was downsized on very short notice. Since this happened the same week he had just undergone a difficult medical procedure, there was no chance for a farewell dinner or even a good-bye cake. Instead, people stopped by his office over the course of several days to talk for a few minutes and to reminisce about ministry projects they had shared. This was more than appropriate since John had made a point of befriending almost everybody in the building on a person-to-person basis, no matter their position. The most moving farewell was when we were pulling away from the building with the last load of files and books. Ed, the night watchman, came out the front door and waved good-bye until we were out of sight, just like an uncle or a brother would. He stood there as a friend, as a colleague, and as a brother in Jesus.

Through the life, death, and resurrection of Jesus, we are all joined to one another. God has imprinted and embedded himself in our common humanity through his Son. The Father has shown us that each of us was loved into being through Jesus, who became flesh of our flesh. Christ knows and loves each of us from the inside out and gives us to one another as a sharing in that same flesh. As baptized Christians, we are part of one family, brothers and sisters in Jesus Christ—even those we have never met. Pope St. John Paul II put it another way:

> The human person has an inherent social dimension which calls a person from the innermost depths of self to *communion* with others and to the *giving* of self to others: "God, who has fatherly

concern for everyone, has willed that all people should form one family and treat one another in a spirit of brotherhood." (*Gaudium et Spes,* 24)[11]

Even so, we are tempted to disown one another in words and deeds. When this happens, it is time to plead with Jesus, "Give me back my sister! Reconcile me to my brother! Make this small part of your family whole again. Anoint us with the strength we need to love each other."

Third: We Are Temples of God's Holy Spirit

When Linda's husband, Clyde, died, she was conflicted about whether to scatter his ashes or bury them in a cemetery. Linda, like many Catholics, was also confused about the Church's stance. When she confided in John, they talked about which choice would be most respectful of Clyde's body. John explained that Linda's husband had truly been a temple of the Holy Spirit. A Catholic cemetery is the resting place for the bodies of the faithful departed—once temples of the Holy Spirit whose souls are now with God—until the day of their resurrection. As such, it is a final and continuing profession of faith (see *Catechism,* 2300).

Linda chose the cemetery, and as Clyde's family assembled there, the consoling presence of Jesus was evident in the priest, the music, and the mutual support that those attending offered one another.

The Blessed Virgin Mary is the best example of a temple of the Holy Spirit. She said yes to the conception of Jesus by the power of the Holy Spirit, and through her presence at the first Pentecost, she became a midwife for the unleashing of the Holy Spirit in the disciples and in all of our personal relationships. Through her many titles, Mary is also the mother of all countries, places, and peoples; God invites us as to respect the Spirit at work in whole groups of people as well.

The concept of Gospel-inspired respect has also been developed through the Church's teaching about the dignity of the human person at every stage of life. In 1983 Cardinal Joseph Bernardin spoke about our need for a "seamless garment," a vision that acknowledges the human dignity of every person and that recognizes temptations to violate others through abortion, capital punishment, assisted suicide, nuclear war, and other acts of social violence. More recently, Pope Francis, by word and example, has encouraged and challenged us to see the presence of the Holy Spirit in others, especially in the poor: "Loving attentiveness is the beginning of a true concern for [the poor]. . . . This entails appreciating the poor [the physically, emotionally, and spiritually poor] in their goodness, in their experience of life, in their culture, and in their ways of living the faith."[12]

Fourth: We Are Unique and Gifted in God's Eyes

One night Therese was awakened by a red glow coming from the bedroom window of her parents' home. The barn had been struck by lightning! Therese ran from room to room, making sure that everyone was awake and out the door while her mother ran after her father, who wanted to save the family car. Fire trucks screeched down the street and careened into the driveway, making quick work of dousing the flames. Unfortunately, all the belongings of Therese's grandparents, stored on the top floor of the barn, had been destroyed.

Therese sat on the steps, shaking. Her grandparents had been poor, blue-collar workers their whole lives. Now they had nothing. But Therese realized that their poverty had never stopped them from opening their home to those in need. Jeannia and Walter had taken in many elderly relatives and either nursed them to health or gave them solace in their final days. When they were in their sixties, they had even sheltered three troubled teenage boys. Having nothing didn't matter to them; only Jesus mattered, and they were who they were because of him.

You might be tempted to define yourself by what you own, by what you do for a living, by your education, or by your online profile. But none of these things define you in God's eyes. Yes, all of these circumstances have shaped you in a particular way, but God is the author of your unique and irreplaceable being. There is no one else just like you. No one has the same gifts, the same story, the same calling. And this is true for every person you encounter. As the psalmist wrote, "For it was you who formed my inward parts; / you knit me together in my mother's womb. / I praise you, for I am fearfully and wonderfully made" (Psalm 139:13-14).

It can be difficult to keep a person's unique goodness in mind as you relate to that person. But think back on the death of a loved one. You knew then that this loved one was irreplaceable. So bring this insight to God when praying for the important people in your daily life right now: "God, I give him to you as if there were no tomorrow. Show me the gifts you have given him so that I can recognize and respond to these gifts according to your love for both of us." Praying this way also sets the stage for the most common way we can respect one another: by listening to the details of another's daily life, as well as the feelings, concerns, and unspoken spiritual needs beneath them. The gift of listening becomes an act of respect, a gift like no other—an opportunity to satisfy our common need to be accepted and appreciated.

Here is a good description of the art of listening:

> We must temporarily abandon our own position in the fullness of attention to the other. We must put ourselves in the other's "boots" and run the risk of never returning to our own. We may lose forever the exact position we had before we listened . . . [so that] at least momentarily we become one with the person speaking. It is only after we have listened in this way that we ourselves can speak words full of meaning.[13]

Fifth: We Are Called to Have Respect for All the Baptized

Our most recent popes have called us to reach out to all the baptized, especially to the more than 75 to 85 percent of Catholics who are not regular churchgoers. In his apostolic exhortation *On Evangelization in the Modern World*, Blessed Paul VI spoke of the need to evangelize the unchurched and the "innumerable people who have been baptized but who live quite outside Christian life."[14] Pope St. John Paul II spoke of the need for a "new evangelization," as did Pope Benedict XVI. This has also been a constant theme for Pope Francis:

> Instead of being just a church that welcomes and receives by keeping the doors open, let us try also to be a church that finds new

roads, that is able to step outside itself and go to those who do not attend Mass, to those who have quit or are indifferent. The ones who quit sometimes do it for reasons that, if properly understood and assessed, can lead to a return. But that takes audacity and courage.[15]

This calls us to respect, rather than judge, where others are in their lives of faith. And respecting our brothers and sisters in faith as part of our very selves leads to a concern about another's spiritual well-being.

Emily's daughter, Jennifer, and future son-in-law, Clark, had just returned from an interview with the deacon who would officiate at their wedding. Clark mentioned that he had been puzzled by how to respond to the deacon's question about what religion he was. "I have no idea!" was his answer. Then he explained that he would have to ask his aunt. "Great!" thought Emily. "My daughter is marrying someone with no religion." The couple stopped by two weeks later on their way to the deacon's next preparation session with big news. "You won't believe it," Clark said. "I found out that I'm Catholic. I even received my First Communion!" Instead of being disappointed that her future son-in-law hadn't attended church since he was a very young child, Emily threw her arms around him. "That's great, Clark. Now we can be Catholics together!"

A call to respect all the baptized is meant to affect parish life as well. In order to answer the call to bring others to Christ, we need relationships with mature Christians who can support us. As we receive that support and love from one another, we are able to go out of the church to evangelize. Such relationships in our parishes expand our hearts, making room for those whom God wants us to reach out to with his love. The New Testament often speaks of the love we must have for our brothers and sisters in Christ. The strength we receive from each other in the body of Christ drives us out the door to understand and listen to the spiritual experiences of friends and family.

Reflection Questions

1. What is your understanding of respect? How has your relationship with Jesus contributed to your thinking and the ways in which you show respect for others or yourself?

2. Which image is most helpful when you consider the worth of yourself and others: "made in the image of God," "brothers and sisters of Jesus," "temples of the Holy Spirit," or some other image? How does this image help you?

3. Who do you know to be a good listener? What is your experience of listening and being listened to? What is it like for you to "listen" to God and to share what you experience in prayer?

4. What does the New Evangelization mean for you? What is your experience of missing and reaching out to all the baptized brothers and sisters who are inactive in their faith?

Skills for Growing in Respect

Sometimes we rush through life, hurrying to work or to the store, passing slower cars on the highway, eating fast food, getting upset if a website opens too slowly. All this rushing can be bothersome. But when it creeps into prayer, rushing is deadly. Rushing prevents us from looking twice at what God is doing in us and in others.

This exercise is based on a prayer by St. John of the Cross (1542–1591), who describes the richness of encountering God in prayer.[16] Read this prayer aloud slowly. Now read it again, letting the images sink into your heart. Now substitute your own words for the underlined words and read it a third time. Then try viewing a video version of this prayer.[17]

O living flame of love
that tenderly wounds my soul
in its deepest center!

O lamps of fire!
In whose splendors
the deep caverns of feeling,
once obscure and blind,
now give forth, so rarely, so exquisitely,
both warmth and light to their Beloved.

How gently and lovingly
you wake in my heart,
where in secret you dwell alone;

and in your sweet breathing,
filled with good and glory,
how tenderly you <u>swell</u> my heart with love.

CHAPTER THREE

FORGIVENESS

The whole Boucher family was gathered in Dad's hospital room. As each grown child approached his deathbed, Dad addressed that son or daughter with a few pithy words, a final farewell for each one. For one son, his pronouncement was, "You have more brains than heart!" For one daughter, he exclaimed, "You have more guts than brains!" When he came to John, he sighed and said, "Why didn't you ever make anything of yourself? I am so disappointed in you." John was crushed by his father's dissatisfaction. And it wasn't the first time that Dad had objected to John's full-time work in Catholic lay ministry.

Dad died a few days later, and a miracle followed his passing. Within forty-eight hours of his death, John received five invitations to teach workshops in various parishes. And within a year, he had a new job, with a $15,000 raise to help support our growing family.

We believe that Dad had changed his mind about his son John. He had forgiven him for "throwing his life away" on Jesus and the Church. Now Dad could see through the merciful eyes of Jesus. And almost every year since then, John has experienced some kind of major physical, spiritual, emotional, or financial blessing on Dad's birthday. Even better than all of this, God has mended their relationship from beyond the grave. Now John can look back on this deathbed encounter without any resentment. Jesus has helped him forgive his father's condemning frustration and many other perceived offenses as well. God has enabled John to embrace mercy as a way of life.

So we encourage each of you to reflect on your experiences with forgiving and being forgiven. Who has forgiven you? What was that like? Who have you been called to forgive? What was your response? Are you satisfied with your ability to forget the times when others have wronged you?

Jesus and Forgiveness

It is difficult to choose a favorite Scripture passage about the mercy of Jesus—there are so many of them! There is the story about the woman who anointed Jesus' feet and then wiped them with her hair (Luke 7:36-50), the incident about the woman caught in adultery (John 7:53–8:11), or the story about the "good thief" who was crucified with Jesus (Luke 23:39-43). It is even more difficult to choose one among the many actions of Jesus that was merciful, such as eating with sinners and tax collectors or forgiving those who put him to death. We could say that Jesus was the personification of God's mercy made manifest in human history. This is the first part of the mystery of forgiveness. It is not that we love Christ first, but rather that he loves and forgives us for all the ways that we reject him, turn from him, and run away from him and from each other. The Greek word for "forgiveness" is *aphienai*, meaning to "loose," "let go," "release," or "omit." It is Christ's free gift.

Jesus forgives because that is his mission. He was sent by the Father so that God's forgiveness would permeate human history. "In this is love, not that we loved God but that he loved us and sent his Son to be the atoning sacrifice for our sins. Beloved, since God loved us so much, we also ought to love one another" (1 John 4:10-11). This gift has changed many hearts, both in the men and women whose stories are told in the Gospels and in countless others through the centuries. Through the grace of God, this forgiveness flows from the heart of Jesus to all of us, drawing us into the joy and unity of the Trinity. The Samaritan woman at the well is a fine example of this joyful response as she raced to tell all the villagers about Jesus—the very same villagers she had been avoiding (John 4:1-42).

Many saints have offered descriptions about the nature of God's forgiveness and mercy. St. John Vianney (1786–1859) wrote, "Our sins are nothing but a grain of sand alongside the great mountain of the mercy of God."[18] St. Francis de Sales (1567–1622) proclaimed, "Where is the foolish person who would think it in his power to commit a sin more than God could forgive."[19] The *Catechism of the Catholic Church* teaches,

> "There is no one, however wicked and guilty, who may not confidently hope for forgiveness, provided his repentance is honest" (*Roman Catechism* I, 11, 5). Christ who died for all men desires that in his Church the gates of forgiveness should always be open to anyone who turns away from sin. (982)

This means that each of us is faced with a life-defining and death-defying choice: will I accept this offer of the unconditional, forgiving love of Christ, or will I reject it?

Surrendering to the Gift of Forgiveness

During his first public interview, published in September 2013, Pope Francis rocked the world with his response to the interviewer's first question, "Who is Jorge Mario Bergoglio?" Pope Francis paused for a few moments and responded, "I am a sinner. This is the most accurate definition. It is not a figure of speech, a literary genre. I am a sinner . . . *I am a sinner whom the Lord has looked upon*" (emphasis added). [20]

Yes! The Christian is someone "whom the Lord has looked upon" with mercy and forgiveness. "As far as the east is from the west, / so far he removes our transgressions from us" (Psalm 103:12). But do you really believe this? Do you know how to accept this gift? Do you surrender to God as a sinner? And do you know how to respond by forgiving yourself in God's presence so that you can be free enough to forgive others?

Let's return to our opening story as an example. John's last encounter with his dad was, unfortunately, all too typical of their relationship. So when it happened, John was challenged to admit his hatred for his father. But John is not alone in facing this kind of situation. Many in modern society experience what is often referred to as the "father wound."[21] Our society suffers from a lack of strong male spiritual role models due to many factors, such as the breakdown of marriage and family life, scandals in the Church, and the false images of manhood fed to us by the media. Many of us are ignored, neglected, abandoned, or even abused by those all-too-human men we call "father." This makes it hard for many of us to accept the gift of forgiveness offered by God the Father or by Jesus Christ (another male). In such situations, the process of experiencing forgiveness is the same.

As John did some studying and praying, he discovered God the Father in the Bible and the irreplaceable affirmation that Jesus received from his Father. The Old Testament refers to God as "Father" only a handful of times. In the New Testament, God is called "Father" over two hundred times.[22] It is also helpful to note that in all four Gospels, Jesus spoke of and prayed to God as "Father," not only "the" Father (as looked upon from a distance), but as "Abba, Father" (as in a close, personal, life-giving relationship; see Mark 14:36). Jesus' prayer reveals that God's fatherhood is greater than any and all of our human images of fatherhood. This challenges us to change—to grow in our understanding of our all-forgiving Father-God. So as John gave his pain to Jesus, it was replaced by a new compassion for his dad, who was an alcoholic and who also had, in turn, a neglectful and abusive alcoholic father. Through God's grace, John could picture all three generations now receiving the love of God the Father and the blessings of Jesus, the Redeemer, and the very mercy of God.

God's Invitations to Forgiveness

The second part of the mystery of forgiveness is that we are called to offer forgiveness to others. To forgive others, we must allow God's Holy Spirit to work through us to love and forgive them. "For if you forgive others their trespasses, your heavenly Father will also forgive you; but if you do not forgive others, neither will your Father forgive your trespasses" (Matthew 6:14-15). This is a bold spiritual truth that is meant to be the measure of every relationship. And if you are thinking that forgiveness is impossible on your own, you are right! Forgiveness can only be your distinguishing mark as a Christian if you are willing to fall on your knees and ask for this gift. Forgiveness and mercy are for those who are open to facing a host of decisions and conscious choices to enter into God's mercy, over and over again, through an ongoing relationship with Jesus Christ lived in the power of the Holy Spirit. Below are some steps you might take.

First: "Forgive" God for Not "Helping" You

Life isn't fair. The reality is that few of us experience life as perfect. We may wish for a better job, home, or spouse, or for better health. And not only may we complain to God about all of this, but we may even be tempted to hold God responsible for the suffering, sadness, and failures we have experienced.

Alicia was struggling with alcohol and sex addictions. She believed that all of her problems were the fault of someone else, even God. She was angry with her parents, who were both alcoholics. She had often prayed this way: "If you really loved me, Jesus, you would take away all my addictions. But you don't!" Then she stopped praying and going to church—until one day a friend challenged her with these words: "I stopped blaming God for the husband that I have a long time ago. Why don't you stop blaming God for your addictions?"

The next week Alicia joined a twelve-step recovery group. Slowly, she began to accept the consequences of her actions and her addictions, and over time she was able to admit that she was angry with God for "watching" her mess up her own life. She forgave her parents for being alcoholics and gave up the rather naïve misconception that she, as well as her parents, would magically get better. And finally, through the Sacrament of Reconciliation, Alicia admitted her own wrongdoing and sorted out all the serious consequences of her behavior.

Second: Be Willing to Believe in God's Unconditional Love and Mercy

Sometimes you may not believe that God the Father, through Jesus Christ, is willing to forgive you. Henry had cheated on his wife, Cynthia, many times, until she was diagnosed with Alzheimer's disease. When this happened, Henry gained a new compassion for her. He stopped cheating, took care of her around the clock for a year, and then visited her daily when she needed nursing-home care. All the while he worried about his sins against Cynthia. He would drive up to his parish church every Sunday and mull over his situation. "I know I need to come back to church," he reasoned, "but then the roof might cave in." So he would leave without going inside.

Then a friend invited Henry to a Bible study for caregivers. And over coffee, this friend suggested that Henry ask God daily to make him "willing to be made willing" to return to Jesus and the Church. As he prayed this way, Henry experienced the voice of God's Spirit whispering about the mercy of Jesus that was meant for him too. Now Henry attends the Bible study occasionally and has made a few more friends in the parish community. Even more people are praying for Henry's return to Sunday liturgies.

Pope Francis talks often about the great mercy of God. We ought to believe what he tells us:

> God never tires of forgiving us; we are the ones who tire of seeking his mercy. Christ, who told us to forgive one another "seventy times seven" (Matthew 18:22), has given us his example: he has forgiven us seventy times seven. Time and time again he bears us on his shoulders. No one can strip us of the dignity bestowed upon us by this boundless and unfailing love. With a tenderness which never disappoints, but is always capable of restoring our joy, he makes it possible for us to lift up our heads and to start anew.[23]

Third: Admit Wrongdoing and Turn toward Jesus

To know and share forgiveness, you must choose God as your Father and see yourself as the prodigal son or daughter. Admit to yourself that you are a sinner and have wounded your relationships with God, with yourself, and with others. Turn yourself inside out and repent. This gift is already yours; all that remains is for you to surrender your life to the Holy Spirit in prayer and renew your baptism by celebrating the Sacrament of Reconciliation.

Interior repentance, according to the *Catechism*,

> is a radical reorientation of our whole life, a return, a conversion to God with all our heart, an end of sin, a turning away from evil, with repugnance toward the evil actions we have committed. At the same time it entails the desire and resolution to change one's life, with hope in God's mercy and trust in the help of his grace. (1431)

As a teenager, Blessed Charles de Foucauld (1858–1916) lost his faith. He served in the French military in North Africa and, after resigning and returning to Paris, underwent a profound conversion. He wrote, "How many are your mercies, O God—mercies yesterday and today, and at every moment of my life, from before my birth, from before time itself began! I am plunged deep in mercies—I drown in them: they cover me, wrapping me around on every side."[24] His words remind us that conversion is not just a once-and-for-all experience. As we grow in Christ, we are called to deeper and deeper levels and kinds of conversion.[25] The United States Conference of Catholic Bishops offers us still another description of conversion:

> Conversion is the change of our lives that comes about through the power of the Holy Spirit. All who accept the Gospel undergo change as we continually put on the mind of Christ by rejecting sin and becoming more faithful disciples in his Church. Unless we undergo conversion, we have not truly accepted the Gospel. . . .
>
> This is crucial: we must be converted—and we must continue to be converted! We must let the Holy Spirit change our lives! We must respond to Jesus Christ. And we must be open to the transforming power of the Holy Spirit who will continue to convert us as we follow Christ. If our faith is alive, it will be aroused again and again as we mature as disciples.[26]

Fourth: Seek Forgiveness from Those You Have Wounded

One night Sheila led a special meeting of St. Bart's parish pastoral council. She had been asked to present plans for an upcoming evangelization project. During the meeting, she was repeatedly interrupted by Frank, who had many questions. At one point she lost her patience and told Frank, "Sit down and shut up!" Others in the room were stunned. Afterward the president of the council spoke to her about her behavior. When she got home that night, Sheila called Frank and asked if she could come over to his house to apologize. When they met face-to-face, she admitted her abusive behavior and wrongdoing; she had embarrassed Frank and did not want to treat him like that again. Sheila asked his forgiveness for the pain she had caused him.

To make restitution for her behavior, Sheila went to the next council meeting and apologized to Frank again and to the entire group. The act of seeking forgiveness connected each person and the whole group to Jesus. Her willingness to repent and ask forgiveness freed the parish council at St. Bart's to move forward in joining eight other parishes in offering an evangelization event. Hundreds of unchurched people and inactive Catholics were brought closer to Jesus Christ through the new unity and peace that prevailed on the council and in the parish.

But what if you repent, seek forgiveness, and try to make amends, and someone still won't forgive you for the hurt you have caused him or her? Then it may be time to step away from the relationship for a while. Stop asking for forgiveness and turn this person and your relationship over to God in prayer as often as needed. Forgiveness is something we enter into according to the graces that are given to us over time.

Fifth: Decide to Forgive Others Who Have Wounded You

At one point after his father's death, John realized that he was holding a lot of things against his dad. He was "stuck," emotionally and spiritually. John's spiritual director suggested following these seven steps to allow God's healing and forgiving love to flow:

1. Admit your anger, resentment, and hurt; then put it into God's hands.

2. Pray daily for the person who hurt you and wish the best for that person.

3. Whenever you become conscious of the pain between you and the other person, decide to forgive him or her.

4. Pray the Scriptures each day, especially those passages that speak of God's unconditional love and mercy.

5. Whenever you receive the Sacraments of Reconciliation and the Eucharist, picture Jesus laying his healing hands upon you and also upon the other person.

6. Thank God for one good thing about this person every day— for example, maybe that person's generosity to the poor.

7. Even before you have any feelings of forgiveness, act in a forgiving, loving, and compassionate way toward the person.

For the next few years, John worked with these suggestions. Then he attended a weekend conference that focused on the healing and forgiving love of God the Father. At one point during the weekend, the speaker invited people who were struggling with forgiveness to raise their hands. Those who were seated around them were asked to stretch out their hands to pray with them. As they prayed, John could see himself as a child of five years old playing on the floor. God the Father reached down to pick him up in his arms. "Isn't he cute?" he said. Then he passed him over to his dad. Then Dad nodded and took John in his arms.

The unconditional healing, mercy, and forgiving love of God the Father overwhelmed John. All his memories of his dad were transformed; the pain was replaced by an abiding understanding and compassion. This also freed him in his relationships with our children.

Today John still uses these suggestions of his spiritual director whenever he faces the possibility that someone might wound or betray him. When someone does hurt him, praying this way brings John peace. He often gains the wisdom to see how God uses difficult people and situations to help him grow in the gifts and fruits of the Holy Spirit.

John believes he has experienced what Pope Francis describes here in his relationships with others:

"I have a dogmatic certainty: God is in every person's life. . . . Even if the life of a person has been a disaster, even if it is destroyed by vices, drugs or anything else—God is in this person's life. You can, you must try to seek God in every human life. Although the life of a person is a land full of thorns and weeds, there is always a space in which the good seed can grow. You have to trust God."[27]

For a very striking example of forgiveness, read the story of Immaculée Ilibagiza, who hid in a small bathroom with seven other women for ninety-one days during the Rwandan genocide in 1994.[28] When she later met the killer of her mother and brother, she said, "I forgive you." Asked why she would ever forgive him, she replied, "Forgiveness is all I have to offer."[29]

Reflection Questions

1. What is it like for you to forgive yourself? What might help you be more compassionate toward yourself?

2. Which is less difficult for you: seeking forgiveness from others or forgiving others? Why?

3. Which of the steps of the suggested forgiveness process listed on page 51 do you find easiest? Which is most challenging? What is your biggest obstacle to forgiving others? What is your experience of dealing with this behavior? How might you become a more forgiving person?

4. What's the most important thing you have learned from this chapter? What might help you most in the future when you feel offended?

Skills for Growing in Forgiveness

Our resistance to forgiving others often flows from patterns of behavior that block God's mercy. Here is an exercise to help you consider patterns of behavior in your life that surface when something goes wrong.

Step One: *Imagine that someone has done something that makes your blood boil, whether it is serious or trivial. You find yourself wanting to react in a very physical way. Now imagine reaching for an imaginary tool that you might use as a weapon. What would it be?*

- a saw (to cut off the relationship)
- a hammer (to insist on what you want)
- pliers (to hang on for dear life)
- a screwdriver (to pin down the other person)
- another tool

Step Two: *Which imaginary tool would you find yourself using? What is it like for you to consider responding this way?*

Step Three: *Lift up your imaginary tool (or get a real one and lift it up to God) as you pray:* "Lord Jesus, I have harmed others with this _____. I am sorry, and I ask your forgiveness. I trust in the Father's mercy, and I promise to seek forgiveness in whatever way you lead me. Amen."

CHAPTER FOUR

GRATITUDE

Therese's suitcase was packed. Car keys, coat, handbag, and road maps were all accounted for. But still she didn't want to leave her sister Susan and her hometown in Massachusetts. It would be another nine months until her next visit. "Let's spend a few more minutes looking at clippings in the family album," Susan offered. And that's when a tiny sentence in a cousin's obituary caught Therese's eye.

"He leaves his sister, Shirley, of Highland Park, New Jersey," Susan read aloud. Therese was amazed. "Wow, that's only five miles from my house." And for the first time in eighteen years, the trip away from Worcester was not consumed by loneliness. It was about moving toward family.

That same week Therese was at Shirley's house, ringing her doorbell. "It's your cousin!" was her greeting. Shirley was shocked. She had just been sitting at her small kitchen table, which was filled with dozens of letters she had written to try and locate relatives. Shirley and Therese experienced a joyful reunion and the beginning of a long friendship. God had answered their mutual need for family and for a little piece of home. They were grateful both to God and to one another.

Who has God given you as gift? For whom are you grateful? What is it like for you to express your gratitude in word and deed? What would it be like to allow God to stretch you so that you can experience gratitude for both the ordinary and the difficult people and events in your life?

Jesus and Gratitude

Jesus was born into a long Jewish tradition of gratitude toward God. This tradition is very evident in the psalms of thanksgiving that he would have known and prayed. Picture him on a spring morning as he takes a few moments away from hammering a table to stretch his arms toward heaven and pray, "I give you thanks, O Lord, with my whole heart; / before the gods I sing your praise; / I bow down toward your holy temple / and give thanks to your name" (Psalm 138:1-2).

Jesus was also raised with a keen awareness of the Exodus story and Moses' joyful song of thanksgiving after Pharaoh's army was swallowed up by the Red Sea (Exodus 15:1-18). He knew the song of Moses' sister, Miriam, as she took up her tambourine: "Sing to the Lord, for he has triumphed gloriously; / horse and rider he has thrown into the sea" (15:21). And perhaps his mother had taught him her own song of praise (Luke 1:46-55).

Against this backdrop of the Jewish tradition of thanksgiving are other examples of Jesus' gratitude. One occurred during his dangerous and final entry into Jerusalem, when he received news that his good friend Lazarus was near death. What would the coming ordeal be like without his good friend by his side? But he did not rush to heal him, sensing that his Father had a different plan—Lazarus would die, but then he would live! Armed with the Father's love, Jesus moved forward to Lazarus' tomb with tears in his eyes. Then, against the reality before him, he spoke out of the depths of gratitude etched into his heart: "'Father, I thank you for having heard me. I knew that you always hear me, but I have said this for the sake of the crowd standing here, so that they may believe that you sent me.' When he had said this, he cried with a loud voice, 'Lazarus, come out!'" (John 11:41-43). Jesus called forth not only Lazarus from the stench of death; he also called everyone—all of us throughout history—to step into his grateful, joyous relationship with his Father.

Another inspiring example of Jesus' gratitude was much more subtle and occurred while he was dying on the cross. As fluid suffocated his lungs and pain emanated from every fiber of his body, Jesus cried out, in the words of Psalm 22, "My God, my God, why have you forsaken me?"(Mark 15:34). At first glance, it seems that Jesus had put aside all hope and gratitude. But as we continue to read the psalm, past the descriptions of intense suffering, such as "all my bones are out of joint; / my heart is like wax" (Psalm 22:14), we discover that it also includes a song of praise: "You who fear the LORD, praise him! / All you offspring of Jacob, glorify him" (22:23). So it is reasonable to conclude that Jesus had the whole psalm in mind as he reached out to his Father.

Surrendering to the Gift of Gratitude

"That was easy for Jesus," you might be tempted to say. "He was the Son of God." We, too, admit an ongoing struggle to be grateful. John is often tempted to be pessimistic about a particular project that he is engaged in bringing to fruition. Therese still has a "Peanuts" plaque that her mother gave her as a teenager that reads, "I have learned to dread one day at a time." So let's begin together by looking at the challenge of thanking God for both the small and the large gifts he showers upon us, for the people he puts in our lives, and for the hints of divine intervention that happen each day.

Eleanor was sitting in John's office with a complaint about a religious education preschool assignment that her daughter Michelle had brought home. The assignment was to draw the gifts that God had given her for Christmas. "Look at this!" Eleanor said as she shoved the paper across John's desk. "God didn't give Michelle anything for Christmas," Eleanor insisted. "My husband did. He worked two jobs to give her all this!"

"Well," John began with caution, "let's imagine that you are Michelle and that you were asked to draw something that you are thankful for during this Christmas season. What would you draw?"

Eleanor thought for a moment. "I'm thankful for good health. Lots of our friends are sick right now."

"And how about your husband?" John asked. "Is he well?"

"Yes, he is, especially compared to last December when he kept getting strep infections."

"Do you suppose that in some way we could say that God gave your husband good health this year? And with the strength that God gave him, your husband could work and buy gifts? And if this is true, then couldn't we say that in some way God brought those toys to Michelle through your husband?"

Eleanor looked thoughtful and replied, "Why, yes. When you put it that way, it's true."

Eleanor's experience echoes the temptation to be shortsighted about the source of all goodness. We might take credit for what we have and who we are. Or we might nurse resentments about what we don't have. In either case, this kind of thinking isolates us from the immensity of God's love. We need to remember the words of St. Paul: "Rejoice always, pray without ceasing, give thanks in all circumstances; for this is the will of God in Christ Jesus" (1 Thessalonians 5:16-18).

This invitation to rejoice may sound foolish. But many believers before us have rejoiced in God's providence despite the worst possible circumstances. In the Book of Nehemiah, the scribe Ezra exhorted the bedraggled Israelites, fresh from captivity, saying, "Do not be grieved, for the joy of the LORD is your strength" (8:10). Edith Stein (1891–1942), also known as St. Teresa Benedicta of the Cross, was first converted through the joy and peace of a friend's widow. St. Damien of Molokai (1840–1889) gave of himself to a desperate, lawless colony of lepers; he built a chapel, dug graves, dressed wounds, and organized farms. "Without the constant presence of our Divine Master upon the altar in my poor chapels," he said, "I never could have persevered casting my lot with the afflicted of Molokai." Later, in 1885, he announced his own case of leprosy, expressing gratitude toward God because he could finally say, "I am one of you" to his people.[30]

God's Invitation to Gratitude

For a Christian, gratitude is not a fleeting or temporary experience. It is also not dependent on feelings or deterred by hardships. If we adopt this attitude, gratitude will naturally flow into our relationships. An expression of gratitude for those we love and for the people in our lives can go a long way in mending relationships and building strong ones. "I am thankful that you are my husband/wife, that you are my son/daughter, that you are my friend" is a way of affirming others and letting them know how much we value them and how much we give thanks to God that they are in our lives. Here are some ways to grow in thankfulness as a way of life.

First: Learn Gratitude from the "Saints" around You

We chose the story of our friend Paul as an example of gratefulness, not because we ran out of stories about canonized saints, but because faith sharing is one way to inspire one another to rejoice.[31] When others share what God has done in their lives, it gives us hope about what is possible for us.

Paul had pulled guard duty on the western perimeter of an army base near Da Nang, South Vietnam. He had a relatively safe job as a cook, but the hell of guerilla warfare and an addiction to drugs had turned his life sour. One night, as he positioned himself to rest against a wall of rice-filled burlap sacks behind the mess tent, the sky suddenly turned fiery red. Surrounded by incoming machine-gun fire and exploding grenades, Paul quickly dropped to the ground. When the shooting had stopped and he had crawled back to his place behind the tent, he noticed that the burlap bags where he had rested his head were peppered with bullet holes.

The hair on Paul's neck stood straight up. Icy fingers of sweat trickled down his spine. Clear as the starting buzzer for a basketball game, he heard God say, "Because I love you, none of these bullets had your name on it." That day Paul was converted to a living faith in Jesus Christ. Since then he has been drug-free and has settled into a happy marriage. This does not mean that Paul doesn't struggle with post-traumatic stress syndrome or the issues beneath his previous addiction. It means that he often looks back at this experience and others as doorways to a life of gratitude. It means that he has made a choice to focus on God's unfolding goodness, strength, and healing.

Do you admire or even notice people in your daily life who are filled with gratitude? We have noticed a pastor who begins every Sunday liturgy by thanking people for coming. Then there is Laura, who says, "I appreciate it!" whenever we do the least little thing for her. We were also struck by a sympathy card we received after the death of a close relative: "I thank God that I knew Harry. He was a kind and prayerful man. I remember the day I lost my job, and his response was to stop and pray with me." The list goes on and on. Our sisters and brothers in faith can offer us countless invitations to thankfulness.

Second: Admit Your Own Ingratitude

Ever had the experience of opening an unattractive Christmas or birthday gift? For Christmas one year, Therese had asked for art supplies. As she opened a long thin box, out came a mysterious object with a wooden handle. "Gee, thanks!" she said with a disappointed look on her face. She did not recognize it as a palette knife until someone explained what the gift was. How often have you been disappointed with the details of your daily life? How often are you more likely to curse or complain instead of seeing the goodness in a situation?

One way to surrender your ingratitude to God is to contemplate the Gospel passage about the ten lepers (Luke 17:11-19). When the nine did not return to thank Jesus after he had healed them, he wondered where they were and why they did not come back to give praise to God. Consider some of their imaginary excuses, taken from an online exercise that we wrote.[32] Which one do you identify with? Do you have even more reasons to harbor ingratitude?

- I'm not sure what really happened. Maybe I imagined the whole thing and the sores will return.

- I got so excited that I just wanted to celebrate at the nearest town square with my friends who were also healed.

- I ran home to show my family. I missed them so much that I couldn't think of anything else.

- Since being healed, I just had so many other important things to do.

- There were a lot of sick and scary people hanging around Jesus. It didn't look like a good place to be for very long.

Ingratitude, like any other failing or sin, must first be acknowledged, along with any of its "companions": self-absorption, jealousy, self-hatred, depression, resentment, and emotional pain. God can help with all of these, but not if we insist on hiding them from him. So an important step is to be vulnerable before God and let Jesus take away the leprosy of ingratitude. And if ingratitude is one of your primary struggles, then we encourage you to do the exercise at the end of the chapter several times over the next few weeks.

Third: Choose a Life of Gratitude and Praise toward God

In 1964 Lorraine divorced her first husband, who was abusive, and then moved in with another man. For the next fifty years, she was away from the Church. Then after both men had died, Lorraine suffered a serious heart attack. While she was in the hospital, she had the opportunity to share her life story with a priest and go to Confession. She glowed with a new gift of gratitude to God. Afterward, as she tried to describe her return to the Eucharist, all she could say was, "It was pretty!"

Lorraine was given a head start on a new chapter of her life, one marked by gratitude and praise. You, too, have many options for embracing a life of thanksgiving, praise, and worship, whether it begins with a new experience or not. But doing so will take some conscious decisions to thank God in prayer.

You could begin by praying with the titles for the Holy Spirit from chapter 1, or you could pray with the titles and names for Jesus. You might also meditate on some of the psalms of thanksgiving and praise: Psalms 23, 47, 84, 100, 138, and 145 through 150. You might sing hymns. Whatever you choose, as you move forward in thanking God for interventions in your life, the Holy Spirit will enlarge your heart, making you capable of praising God with new joy.

It is also important to choose worship and thanksgiving along with the whole body of Christ. During the preface of the Eucharistic Prayer of the Mass, the priest says, "Let us give thanks to the Lord our God," and the congregants respond, "It is right and just." The *Catechism of the Catholic Church* says that in this part of the Mass, "the Church gives thanks to the Father, through

Christ, in the Holy Spirit, for all his works: creation, redemption, and sanctification. The whole community thus joins in the unending praise that the Church in heaven, the angels and all the saints, sing to the thrice-holy God" (1352). Choosing praise is one of our reasons for attending the daily Eucharistic liturgies, where we can offer the sacrifice of praise together.

Finally, be inspired by an upbeat Hebrew song called "Dayenu," sung during Passover Seders since the Middle Ages. Each verse acknowledges something God has done and comes to an inspiring conclusion. "If He would've split the sea for us, and not let us through it on dry land, it would've been enough for us. / If He would've let us through it on dry land, and not drowned our enemies in it, it would've been enough for us."[33] Singing this song helps us reflect on events in our daily lives as singular manifestations of God's love. It also challenges us: what is "enough" for those of us who follow Christ?

Fourth: Acknowledge Your Gifts and Search Out the Gifts of Others

Part of the Facebook phenomenon is the abundance of light-hearted quizzes offered by websites like PlayBuzz and BuzzFeed. A quiz might ask, "What word best describes you?" or "Which one of Jesus' disciples are you?" Then people compare their results on Facebook. These quizzes appeal to our fascination with who we are and the reality of how others see us. The answers have been a fun way for Therese to compare childhood experiences with her sisters and cousins.

John learned about some of his gifts through an instrument called the *Catholic Spiritual Gifts Inventory*.[34] It highlighted his ability to lead and to empower others in ministry projects. Therese gained insights about herself by reading a book called *Sealed Orders* by Agnes Sanford, in which the author compared her gifts of writing, art, research, and healing to instruments in an orchestra that blend together according to the conductor's directions.[35] But it is only in recent years that we have both learned how to put all of our gifts together in order to serve the Church. Now we enjoy learning about the many saints whose deep friendships and complementary gifts helped them to work together to build God's kingdom: Sts. Rose of Lima and Martin de Porres; Sts. Ignatius Loyola and Francis Xavier; Sts. Vincent de Paul and Louise de Marillac; and Sts. Marianne Cope and Damien de Veuster.

Studying the lives of such saints helps us to realize that each believer's gifts are meant to be appreciated and developed in the context of the mix of gifts that occur in a marriage, a friendship, a family, or a ministry group. When we view gifts from this perspective, we are modeling the relationships at the heart of the Trinity and we are relying on each other to follow Jesus. Here are some underlying attitudes that make this possible:

- Each person has a bouquet of gifts that takes time to nurture, and appreciating this truth gives us patience with others. Each person's combination of gifts is unlike anyone else's, and appreciating this protects us from envy.

- Noticing gifts in others and acknowledging them with a simple "thank you" builds our relationships, because then what we say and do is "rooted and grounded in love" (Ephesians 3:17). Statements like "Thank you for cooking supper" or "Thanks for picking up the dry cleaning" are important. We will say more about this in the chapter about affirming others.

- Your gifts belong to others. It is when you use them in service to others that these gifts grow and glorify God. When Therese thanks John for listening to a problem, she appreciates his gift of listening, which he has given her at that moment.

- Limitations and faults can shed light on our gifts. They are often the bad side of something good. For example, Therese gets agitated when a gathering or meeting does not start on time. This is because she has task-oriented gifts and has a lot of respect for people's time.

Fifth: Cultivate Gratitude for Those You Serve

Jesus went out of his way to dine with sinners, tax collectors, and prostitutes. He also touched lepers and did not shy away from possessed or mentally ill people. When asked why he did this, Jesus said to them, "Those who are well have no need of a physician, but those who are sick; I have come to call not the righteous but sinners" (Mark 2:17). We believe that Jesus' actions challenge us to seek out the poor and those in need and serve them with real love, affection, and gratitude.

When we moved and joined the same inner-city parish where we had served as young adults, we were pleased that the compassion of Jesus for those in need was still very much alive there.

A center had been built that serves breakfast each day, and one family had established an orphanage in Haiti. Our pastor, Fr. John Madden, says he experiences gratitude in his service to the poor because in such relationships, ultimately, we have only ourselves to offer, not our goods and services. "We do this better on some days than on others." In addition, these relationships open our eyes and our hearts to our own poverty. "I see the Lord and know the always free and unconditional love God has for us. And there is no greater call than to live the gospel of Jesus, who displays a preferential love for the poor."[36]

Whom do you serve? Is it your spouse, your children, your co-workers, or those struggling with material or spiritual poverty? In these relationships, we can give of ourselves, as difficult as that may be sometimes. And as we serve others with love, affection, and gratitude, we are able to acknowledge that we are in need as well.

What kinds of poverty have you embraced for the sake of the gospel? What corporal or spiritual works of mercy has God challenged you to do in the name of Jesus? We are certain that as you respond to God through these works of mercy, you will experience the gift of gratitude in new and deeper ways for the people you serve and for what God empowers you to do.

Reflection Questions

1. When have you been grateful to God? Whom are you grateful for in your life? In what ways have you expressed your gratitude to and about this person?

2. When you think about the nine lepers who were healed but did not return to Jesus, what comes to mind? How are you similar to one of these lepers? What has been your experience of ingratitude toward God? How could you move away from this behavior?

3. Think about a group of people to whom you belong: a family, a working group, a collection of friends. List the people in the group, including yourself. What are some of the gifts that you have noticed in individuals? What could you do to acknowledge some of these gifts?

4. In what ways have you experienced poverty? Where was God in this experience? How are you challenged to grateful service for someone struggling with poverty?

5. What is one insight you have gained from this chapter? How could you apply it to your daily life? How could you surrender more fully to the gifts of joy and gratitude?

Skills for Growing in Gratitude

St. Paul begins many of his epistles by thanking God for his listeners, even when he is addressing serious problems in the community (see Romans 1:8; 1 Corinthians 1:4; Ephesians 1:16; and Philippians 1:3). How often do you consider the good qualities of the people around you?

Here is an exercise, called "story webbing," that will expand your ability to experience gratitude.

Step One: *Think of someone with whom you have a positive relationship. Draw a circle with his or her name inside it. Then draw lines radiating from the circle, listing each good quality along each line. Draw as many lines as needed. Then thank God for this person and for each good quality. Consider thanking this person for one of their good qualities this week.*

Step Two: *Think of someone whom you experience as difficult. Then draw this same circle and list his or her good qualities along radiating lines. This will be challenging. "Bad" qualities may surface first, but ask the Lord to show you how he sees this person. Then ask God's forgiveness for any harm you have done to this person, and thank him for this person and for mending your heart. End with this psalm:*

> Great is the LORD, and greatly to be praised;
>   his greatness is unsearchable. . . .
> The LORD is faithful in all his words,
>   and gracious in all his deeds.
> The LORD upholds all who are falling,
>   and raises up all who are bowed down.
> The eyes of all look to you,
>   and you give them their food in due season.
> You open your hand,
>   satisfying the desire of every living thing.
> (Psalm 145:3, 13-16)

CHAPTER FIVE

AFFIRMING OTHERS

It's easy to remember the first time that Therese complimented John in front of his mother. It was an autumn day. We had driven over a hundred miles, complete with construction detours and hours of bumper-to-bumper traffic. Our three pre-schoolers were beyond cranky when we arrived at his parents' house. John took the kids out in the yard for a while. Then he lined them up on the couch to read a book about animals. His flair for the dramatic kicked in, and the kids were enthralled. "John, you really brought those animals to life and helped all the children settle down. That was great—thank you!" Therese called out from the kitchen.

John's mother was flabbergasted. She teased us by patting herself on the back and exclaiming, "Boy, am I wonderful! Call the television studio and have the President come and give me a medal!" Offering and receiving affirmation was something foreign to Mom. She was taught that compliments would make a person have a "swelled head." She was more accustomed to being ignored for all that she did. For us, too, it was a new skill that flowed from learning how to be grateful for each other and then trying to express that gratitude to strengthen our marriage.

What were some of your key experiences of being affirmed by parents, teachers, or relatives as you were growing up or in your early adulthood? Or perhaps you only remember episodes of destructive criticism, sarcasm, bullying, or negative humor directed at you by significant people in your life. Let's take a look at the many ways that Jesus encouraged and affirmed those around him and the way he encourages those who follow him today. Then we will consider ways to act out the gift of gratitude through affirming speech.

Jesus and Affirming Others

Jesus Christ is the living Word, the Word that transforms us (John 1:1-4). Scripture uses the word *dabar* (Hebrew) or *logos* (Greek) for "word" or "event" to describe Jesus and the first joyful coming of Christ at Christmas: "When the angels had left them and gone into heaven, the shepherds said to one another, 'Let us go now to Bethlehem and see *this thing* [*dabar/logos*—word/event] *that has taken place*, which the Lord has made known to us" (Luke 2:15, emphasis added).

Jesus is the climax of every word from God in the Old Testament, beginning with the Father's creative, affirming, and life-giving words: "Then God said, 'Let us make humankind in our image, according to our likeness'" (Genesis 1:26). God also spoke to Noah, Abraham, Moses, and the prophets, affirming his covenant love for the Hebrew people. As he said through the prophet Jeremiah, "This is the covenant that I will make with the house of Israel after those days, says the LORD: I will put my law within them, and I will write it on their hearts; and I will be their God, and they shall be my people" (31:33). And so God's word unfolded in salvation history, touching the depths of the human heart for all time.

Then Jesus was sent as the final Word of God made flesh to free us from our rebellion and our brokenness and lead us home to God the Father (John 1:1-14). At his baptism in the Jordan River, "the heaven was opened, and the Holy Spirit descended upon him in bodily form like a dove. And a voice came from heaven, 'You are my Son, the Beloved; with you I am well pleased'" (Luke 3:21-22). Jesus, in turn, spoke words of encouragement and affirmation to those around him. When Simon Peter saw the miraculous catch of fish on the lake of Gennesaret, "he fell down at Jesus' knees, saying, 'Go away from me, Lord, for I am a sinful man!' . . . Then Jesus said to Simon, 'Do not be afraid; from now on you will be catching people.' When they had brought their boats to shore, they left everything and followed him" (5:8, 10-11).

We hear God's affirming voice at Simon the Pharisee's home when a woman washed Jesus' feet with her tears and dried them with her hair. Then Jesus said to the woman, "Your faith has saved you; go in peace" (Luke 7:50). We hear another affirmation when a Roman centurion asked Jesus to heal his servant and said, "Lord, I am not worthy to have you come under my roof; but only speak the word, and my servant will be healed" (Matthew 8:8). Jesus replied, "'Truly I tell you, in no one in Israel have I found such faith. . . . Go; let it be done for you according to your faith.' And the servant was healed in that hour" (Matthew 8:10, 13).

St. Paul followed Jesus' lead through the many greetings he offered at the beginning of his letters. He referred to his listeners as "God's beloved" (Romans 1:7). In 1 Corinthians 1:4, Philippians 1:3, and Colossians 1:3, he thanked God for the goodness of his followers. How can we do less when we greet one another?

Surrendering to the Gift of Affirmation

When John went off to college, he hoped to find a good wife and graduate with good grades so that he could land a job making good money. By sophomore year, he realized that these hopes would be much harder to come by than he had ever imagined. Emptiness and loneliness followed. No combination of work and partying filled the void. During his junior year, he began to plan a painless way to commit suicide, until Jack invited him to go on an Antioch Weekend retreat. He accepted, willing to give life one last chance.

On Saturday night of the weekend, he spoke to a priest on the retreat team, who gave him a copy of the New Testament with the Psalms and suggested that he go to the chapel and ask God for what he needed to be happy. As he sat before the Blessed Sacrament, he opened the Scriptures and his eyes fell upon the first line of Psalm 23: "The LORD is my shepherd, I shall not want." John thought, "I want all kinds of things, but how, God, how?" He wept in pain until deep down inside, he sensed God saying to him, "I love you just the way you are. You don't have to be the best. You don't have to be perfect or in control. Just let me love you. I'll change whatever needs changing in you." John's problems didn't clear up overnight, but ever since then he has learned to search out God's affirming voice in his life. Ever since then, the living Word, who is Jesus, has become the first and last word in his life.

Debby is another example of someone who has heard the affirming words of Jesus. She had run away from physically abusive parents and then worked as a prostitute to support herself. In her mid-thirties, while she was waitressing in a local diner, a woman from our parish invited her to our Bible study. She came for weeks and then months, eyes darting around, back glued to the far wall, never speaking a word to anyone. Finally, one night after we had studied the story about the sinful woman who washed Jesus' feet (Luke 7:36-50), Debby asked to speak to John. "This words," she explained in her broken English, "they about me!" She had heard God's voice, and now she was home. Little by little Debby's life began to change. She sat down during our studies and even smiled from time to time. The Holy Spirit spoke to her in many ways, especially through the acceptance of the members of our group. About a year later, Debby announced that she wanted to follow Jesus by becoming Catholic.

God's Invitation to Affirm Others

You, too, can be strengthened by the affirming word of Father, Son, and Spirit. And from that strength, you can affirm others in their goodness by seeing them do good things and encouraging them to continue doing the good. It is a simple way to love like Christ in daily life, a way of virtue that echoes God's word to others. Blessed Teresa of Calcutta (1910–1997) wrote, "There are many people who can do big things, but there are very few people who will do the little things [God wants most]."[37] Here are some ways to be instruments of God's affirming words to others.

First: Affirmation Is a Gift

When John first noticed Bob's capacity to affirm and encourage others, he became uncomfortable and irritated, even angry.

This made no sense. Bob hadn't done anything wrong. So John brought the matter to his spiritual director. Fr. Ray helped John realize that he was envious of Bob's ability to connect with others through gifts of affirmation and encouragement. John had experienced lots of criticism and few compliments in his life. It was a huge blind spot for him. How could affirmation like Bob's be genuine? Wasn't it just flattery? How could anyone really see people that way? It was time to repent of his jealousy toward Bob's gifts. For his penance, Fr. Ray told John to pay attention to how Bob used his gifts and learn ways to affirm others.

It took a lot of work to resist the temptation to destroy others through sarcasm, negative humor, gossip, and destructive criticism. John prayed with James 3 for a long time: "How great a forest is set ablaze by a small fire! And the tongue is a fire. . . . With it we bless the Lord and Father, and with it we curse those who are made in the likeness of God" (verses 5-6, 9). John also began to ask God to fill the void by giving him the gift of encouragement for others when he felt like criticizing them.

Second: Monitor Thoughts about Yourself and Others

Therese was excited about bringing our two young grandchildren to Mass at an outdoor shrine at the top of a hill near their house. All three were settled onto the rustic wooden benches when the priest began his homily. Then Alexandra leaned over and whispered, "Memere, I have to go to the bathroom."

"Oh no," thought Therese. "I didn't bring them there first. So now I don't even know if this is true or if I am a victim of a preschool scam. How could I be so stupid?"

So off they went down the long hill to the retreat center, shaving several minutes off the Mass. As the hymns from the loudspeakers floated overhead during their climb back up to the liturgy, Therese thought, "We will miss too much! And I have taught them nothing." So she tried to salvage a bit of worship by singing along with the congregation at the top of the hill. Paige squeezed her hand and said, "God must be very proud of you, Memere!" Her little voice was a jolt. "How could God be proud of me or love me right now?" Therese asked herself. "I didn't even attend a whole Mass!"

Moments when things go wrong, and even moments when you sin, are times when the Holy Spirit can nudge you to stop unhealthy, condemning thoughts. Choose instead the living word of God by interspersing your thoughts with short prayers or a few words from a favorite hymn. Engage in an honest conversation with Jesus. Let God convert your mind and heart. Let God remind you that you (and others) are made in his image and likeness, that you are brothers and sisters of Jesus Christ, and that you are temples of the Holy Spirit.

Choose more gospel-oriented ways to talk to yourself about mistakes and sins. "You got in another car accident, you child of God!" "You forgot the time of your appointment, you daughter of the Father!" "You hurt your spouse's feelings by your belittling remarks, you brother of Jesus!" This type of interior self-talk is much more in line with our deepest identity as sinners who are saved by God's mercy in Jesus Christ. And by talking to yourself in this way, you are much more likely to extend it to others.

Third: Learn How to Accept Compliments

Compliments are unique opportunities for giving and receiving affirmation. And your attitude toward them can be a good indicator of the ways in which the good news of God's love and forgiveness has filtered into your relationships.

First, let's look at receiving compliments. Do you reject compliments or encouragement because of a low self-image? If so, when someone compliments you about what you have done or who you are, you might be tempted to say things like "It wasn't much" or "I don't deserve it." When that happens, you are refusing a gift and giving in to self-hate. Instead, you might reply, "Thank you for noticing" or "How good of you to say so!" A simple "Thank you" is even better, followed by a silent "Thank you" to God for giving you whatever the person has noticed. Church history is filled with humble people—St. André Bessette (1845–1937) among them—who attributed the good within them to God while accepting their own shortcomings as all the more reason to turn to him.

Do you know the difference between flattery and real affirmation? Flattery is superficial, insincere praise, not based on truth or reality. Flattery puffs up while affirming words build up. Flattery and false pride go hand in hand, leading a person to think that he or she is better, smarter, or holier than others. C. S. Lewis has observed, "As long as you are proud you cannot know God. A proud man is always looking down on things and people; and, of course, as long as you are looking down, you cannot see something that is above you."[38] So avoid taking flattery seriously, and guard against false pride.

The Holy Spirit calls you, as a disciple of Jesus Christ, to speak in ways that affirm others in their goodness and encourage them to continue to do the good. You can recognize and develop the skill of affirming speech by cultivating the virtues of tenderness and gentleness toward others. You might keep a spiritual journal in order to review underlying patterns in your conversations and relationships. You might give close friends and relatives permission to remind you when you refuse compliments or slip into negative remarks. If all of this seems to be too difficult, you might also consider seeking guidance or professional help with issues of self-worth and self-esteem.

Fourth: Encourage Others with Compassion

Julie took a course called "The History of Religion in America." She had hoped that the class would include insights about the Catholic Church. Instead, whenever Mr. Graff spoke about historical events related to the Church, he belittled Catholics. Julie was disturbed about his approach and tried arguing with him. But that did not help anyone.

So Julie prayed and asked God to show her one good thing about Mr. Graff. It took a while. But then she noticed that he always used primary documents—eyewitness accounts, letters, and writings of individuals in a particular historical period. These documents brought the class to life. So every now and then, Julie thanked her teacher for a particular document and shared how reading it had helped her realize how the people in that era might have felt and thought. Over time, they grew in respect for each other.

Retreat master and spiritual director Fr. Thomas Dubay describes this practice of seeking out the good in others and affirming what we find: "To care is to jump into the other's skin. It is to become the other in mind and heart, to live the other's interests. To care is to become one's brother, one's sister."[39]

So how do we begin? First, ask Jesus to show you one good thing about someone you relate to in a significant way so that you have the groundwork for encouraging that person. It doesn't matter whether you have a positive or a negative relationship with that person.

Second, resolve to tell this person about this quality the next time he or she exhibits such goodness.

Third, thank God for what you discover. As you see more good things, thank God for each of these attributes as well.

Fourth, add this person to your daily intentions, especially if your relationship needs improvement.

Fifth, ask God to fulfill his or her needs, especially the most pressing spiritual needs.

Fifth: Moving toward Forbearance

When you notice another's faults, ask yourself how you might have the same fault. Many of us detest in others the very things we are struggling with ourselves. The fact is that unacceptable behavior is often easier to see in someone else, and when we notice it in others, it gives us the hope that we can distance ourselves from that behavior. Instead of focusing on the fault, God invites us to choose forbearance, which we will explore in a later chapter. For now, we are concentrating on affirming others and letting go of judging a person or their motives. Remember, only God knows the depths of another's heart.

Try to compliment another person for the good that he or she is doing. You might just inspire this person to live up to the image of their best selves and their baptismal dignity in Jesus Christ. Be sure to offer meaningful and specific compliments that touch upon the good qualities you notice. This is easier to understand with a physical example. "You look good with that haircut" compliments the person while "What a great haircut!" compliments the stylist. Note how St. Paul often pointed out how faithful people were and the good they were doing, even before he corrected them. His Letter to Philemon is a good example of affirming speech: "When I remember you in my prayers, I always thank my God because I hear of your love for all the saints and your faith toward the Lord Jesus. I pray that the sharing of your faith may become effective when you perceive all the good that we may do for Christ" (1:4-6).

One tragic characteristic of modern society is our incapacity to express positive admiration and affection for the people we love and respect, especially in groups. Instead, we often take them for granted and might use "negative humor." Author Jeanne Kun describes this problem:

> Negative humor often takes a jab at someone's mistakes, weaknesses, or eccentricities. Often it may be intended to be affectionate and familiar, a way of kidding someone with tongue in cheek or even of giving a backhanded compliment. . . . It is frequently infected with jealousy, competitiveness, or one-upmanship. And, what appears on the surface as harmless and playful jesting can

lead to insecurity in our relationships. Being criticized or "put down" under the cloak of a joke eventually makes us feel unsure of ourselves and what others think of us.[40]

One of the most challenging occasions for examining our patterns of speech and the attitudes behind them is conversation in small groups. When we are gathered in a group, someone often slips into negative remarks, gossip, or complaining about others. So invite others to speak words of affirmation and compassion by modeling it yourself.

Sixth: Move beyond Silence

Jesus said, "You have heard that it was said to those of ancient times, 'You shall not murder'; . . . But I say to you that if you are angry with a brother or sister, you will be liable to judgment" (Matthew 5:21-22). Quoting that passage, Pope Francis added,

> And whoever insults his brother, kills him in his heart, whoever hates his brother, kills his brother in his heart; whoever gossips against his brother, kills him in his heart. Maybe we are not conscious of it, and then we talk, 'we write off' this person or that, we speak ill of this or that. . . . And this is killing our brother.[41]

But being silent when we hear gossip or other malicious remarks is not always a solution. All too often our silence in the face of such behavior can be interpreted as our agreement. Here are some possible actions you might take in a group that is speaking about others without the compassion of Jesus:

- Help others to realize that none of us is perfect. We all have faults. You might admit something similar about yourself in a general way.

- Give the person being attacked the benefit of the doubt, and express this aloud. Question if the person's actions have been misunderstood or misinterpreted by others.

- Mention something positive that you admire about the person.

- Invite the group to stop and pray for the person to receive God's love.

- If you cannot do any of the above, do not participate in the conversation. Walk away.

When the Pharisees brought to Jesus a woman caught in adultery, he stooped down, drew in the sand, and said, "'Let anyone among you who is without sin be the first to throw a stone at her.' . . . When they heard it, they went away, one by one, beginning with the elders" (John 8:7, 9).

Changing the behavior of a group of people is not the goal. Your goal is to act with integrity and compassion toward both those present and those who are not present. The challenge is to do so in the light of the good news of Jesus Christ, which is meant for all people.

Reflection Questions

1. What inspires you about the way in which Jesus spoke to those in need of encouragement, such as Nicodemus, St. Peter, or Mary Magdalene when she met Jesus after the resurrection?

2. What is your experience of being complimented or being given credit for something good?

3. What helps you move away from self-criticism and into God's mercy for you? How has God mended your relationship with yourself?

4. In Matthew 15:11, Jesus points out the great power of the human voice—either to speak words that affirm others or to utter words that destroy others and defile the speaker. When have you used affirming words with others? What has been the result? What have you noticed about the effects on your relationships?

Skills for Growing in Affirming Others

This exercise, an "Affirmation in Daily Life," is based on the Ignatian examen. Take five to ten minutes at the end of each day to review how you have affirmed, encouraged, or strengthened others. Choose a quiet place where you will not be disturbed.

Step One: *Ask the Holy Spirit to give you the grace and courage to review your day.*

Step Two: *Scroll through the events of the day and list up to three or four conversations you had. Then, for each one, ask: "How did another's words or actions affirm me? How did I affirm that person?"*

Step Three: *Thank God for the people who affirmed or encouraged you.*

Step Four: *Ask God to forgive you for ways in which you hurt or failed to affirm another.*

Step Five: *Ask God to use your words and actions to affirm others tomorrow.*

Close with the Prayer of St. Francis:

> Lord, make me an instrument of Your peace;
> Where there is hatred, let me sow love;
> Where there is injury, pardon;
> Where there is error, truth;
> Where there is doubt, faith;
> Where there is despair, hope;
> Where there is darkness, light;
> And where there is sadness, joy.

O Divine Master,
Grant that I may not so much seek
To be consoled as to console;
To be understood as to understand;
To be loved as to love.
For it is in giving that we receive;
It is in pardoning that we are pardoned;
And it is in dying that we are born to eternal life.

CHAPTER SIX

PATIENCE AND FORBEARANCE

Morning Mass was over. Therese looked forward to walking down the steps of the church and off to a nearby bus stop with her mom. But Claire was uneasy about something. "What is it, Mom?" Therese asked. "Oh, I asked God to help me put up with my co-worker, Penny. She's got a nervous cough and an uncanny knack for chatting when I'm behind in my work. And to make matters worse, the only answer I get from God is to make her my best friend."

We can only assume that Mom took God's word to heart and befriended Penny. Maybe she stopped to listen more often or started eating lunch with her. We don't know how she did it, but when Claire died, Penny was heartbroken. "Claire was my best friend," she told us. Penny was so grateful for their relationship that after Claire's untimely death, she began visiting Claire's mom, Jeannia, once a month with a bag of goodies. Month after month and year after year, Penny drove to Jeannia's nursing home until Jeannia died twelve years later.

Do you find yourself "putting up" with someone? Do you sometimes avoid people rather than relate to them? In our example, Claire moved beyond the temptation to reject, or even merely tolerate, her co-worker. She chose forbearance, which involves a movement of the heart, a God-given ability to "bear one another's burdens, and in this way . . . fulfill the law of Christ" (Galatians 6:2).

Jesus and Forbearance

Jesus had an immense capacity to "bear with" groups of needy people who sought him out for help. He took the time to embrace and bless a group of infants being thrust at him by their clamoring mothers (Luke 18:15-17). Another time, after a weary Jesus and his disciples had crossed the water to be alone, a sizable crowd followed on foot. Instead of being annoyed, "he had compassion for them, because they were like sheep without a shepherd; and he began to teach them many things" (Mark 6:34). And when a blind beggar shouted, "Son of David, have mercy on me!" even after onlookers tried to silence him (Luke 18:39), Jesus stopped, asked the man what he wanted, and healed him. (And David was the king who enjoyed God's forbearance when he stole the wife of Uriah!)

Forbearance is closely related to the gift of longsuffering, which means resisting the tendency to get angry over a period of time. The whole Gospel portrait of Jesus fits this description, especially in the Gospel of Mark, where the disciples often misunderstood Jesus.

Forbearance is also a close companion of patience. In the Gospels, Jesus listened to his followers and then explained himself to them on countless occasions. Here are some striking examples of his patience and forbearance from the Gospel of Mark:

- After Jesus had healed many while staying at Peter's house, the disciples found Jesus off by himself praying, and they urged him to return. Instead, he replied, "Let us go on to the neighboring towns, so that I may proclaim the message there also"

(1:38). They did not seem to understand either why he prayed so much or why he couldn't stay in one place.

- When Jesus was transfigured before Peter, James, and John, Peter suggested building a prayer tent. But then they heard a voice instead urging them to listen (9:2-8).

- Jesus interrupted his nightly prayer to check on the apostles, who were rowing against a strong wind on the Sea of Galilee. He meant to pass by on the water, but they saw him and were terrified. Jesus encouraged them, saying, "Take heart, it is I; do not be afraid" (6:50). Not only did the disciples lack understanding, Mark says, but "their hearts were hardened" (6:52). Still, Jesus rescued them and loved them with real affection.

- When the disciples failed to understand Jesus' reference to the "yeast of the Pharisees," he asked them, "Are your hearts hardened?" (8:15, 17).

Surrendering to the Gifts of Patience and Forbearance

It is easy to imagine St. Joseph teaching Jesus about forbearance in light of Matthew's story about Jesus' conception (1:18-24). We are told that Joseph was a righteous person who struggled with the news of Mary's pregnancy. Since they were already betrothed and had made a formal agreement to marry, Joseph had the right to demand a severe punishment. But the Gospel tells us that he was "unwilling to expose her to public disgrace"

(Matthew 1:19). How unlike so many of us who gossip as freely as we breathe, or who watch television programs that tear apart a person's character! How merciful and forbearing Joseph was! Instead of choosing disgrace and punishment for Mary, Joseph decided on a quiet divorce. But even then, as he surrendered Mary's situation to God, an angel appeared to him in a dream: "Do not be afraid to take Mary as your wife" (1:20). And so, "When Joseph awoke from sleep, he did as the angel of the Lord commanded" (1:24). Joseph accepted Jesus and Mary with unconditional love.

John learned a lot about forbearance when he was hired as the director of a large religious education program at a parish. It did not take long to realize that a part-time grade-level coordinator named Bill had been passed over for the director's job and was very angry about the situation. John knew that working with Bill would be a great challenge. Treating him as just another parish employee or as a subordinate would not work. So John decided to treat Bill as a full partner in ministry and as a brother in the Lord Jesus. He used their one-on-one planning meetings as an opportunity to pray and share their faith together as well as to discuss the business at hand. For the first year, Bill resisted nearly every suggestion that John offered about how to serve more effectively and was either hostile or passive-aggressive.

Then, during the second year of their shared ministry, Bill made a serious mistake that involved purchasing materials for his grade levels. John spoke with the pastor and parish administrator on Bill's behalf, pointing out that there were no clear written guidelines about acceptable purchases of this type or about limits for reimbursement. John suggested that such guidelines be put in writing for all the parish's ministries. In addition, John asked that Bill's error be forgiven and that Bill be reimbursed.

Later in that same year, Bill made another mistake, this time involving an e-mail exchange with a complaining parishioner and others in the diocese. Once again, John met with the pastor to smooth out the brouhaha that followed and to intercede for Bill, suggesting that unspoken protocols be written down and communicated to everyone on the parish staff. Then John talked with Bill about his good intentions in writing the e-mail and about his ignorance of diocesan protocols for dealing with complaints. He also prayed with him.

By this point, Bill realized that John was not intent on destroying him, and his whole attitude changed. Now Bill understands that ministry is not about looking for mistakes. Ministry is about looking for the good that people do and encouraging them through the presence of Jesus in our midst. Finally, John and Bill could be friends and enjoy many years of service together.

God's Invitations to Patience and Forbearance

One author defines forbearance this way: "The ability to patiently endure lasting offenses or hardships, forbearance is one of the hardest virtues to practice because it requires you to respond with patience and love, over and over, to the same situation [or person] over a long period of time."[42] We would add that forbearance, or the lack of it, is rooted in the quality of our relationships—whether it is about Jesus relating to the crowds, the needy, or his disciples, or whether it is about a relationship with a spouse, parent, friend, or ourselves. Here are some suggestions for entering into God's mercy.

First: Meekness, Patience, Humility, and Forbearance

"Meekness was the method that Jesus used with the apostles," wrote St. John Bosco (1815–1888). "He put up with their ignorance and roughness and even their infidelity. He treated sinners with kindness and affection that caused some to be shocked, others to be scandalized, and still others to gain hope in God's mercy. Thus, he bade us to be gentle and humble of heart."[43]

You might not use the word "meekness," but it is a good description of Christ and the saints as they related to people and situations beyond their control. Think of Jesus before Pilate and the chief priests (Matthew 27:11-13). Remember St. Thérèse of Lisieux, who was known for her disarming smile even when another sister was being unkind to her. Then there is St. Damien of Molokai, who experienced decades of frustration as he dealt with Church and government officials to get help for his lepers.

For a long time, we experienced isolation and confusion about one whole branch of John's family who had cut themselves off from siblings and cousins in the 1950s. It was only a few years ago that John was successful in reaching out to one first cousin through Facebook. None of us know what family situation caused the break. But now as we put the bits and pieces together, we can choose forbearance toward parents, aunts, and uncles in a more conscious way. Now we can embrace this suffering together and rebuild.

As you move forward in bearing with difficulties, both your own and those of others, you will find it necessary to face a flood of emotions that cascade down on top of each other like a small avalanche. When you do, Jesus invites you to examine yourself first. He invites you to remove the log from your own eye rather than concentrating on the speck in your neighbor's eye (Matthew 7:1-5). And when this too seems impossible, take heart. God does not invite you to face your faults and inadequacies without first giving you what you need to do so. Whether it is patience or meekness that is the first step for you, the rest will follow as you continue down the path of forbearance.

These words from St. Paul can help:

> As God's chosen ones, holy and beloved, clothe yourselves with compassion, kindness, humility, meekness, and patience. Bear with one another and, if anyone has a complaint against another, forgive each other. . . . Above all, clothe yourselves with love, which binds everything together in perfect harmony. (Colossians 3:12-14)

Second: Who Owes Me What?

One definition of forbearance refers back to the Greek word *ano-che*, which means "a holding back" when someone owes a debt. This definition points toward one of the obstacles to experiencing forbearance. You may be thinking that someone owes you acceptance and respect at every turn in a relationship. One example of this phenomenon may be your attitude toward other drivers on the road. Do you expect everyone to drive by the rules at all times? Do you get angry when they don't? When you think this way, you are treating others as either gods, who should be perfect, or as demons, who are evil incarnate. Neither extreme is based in the good news of Jesus Christ, who has come to redeem all of us. Neither attitude brings us any closer to God's unconditional love for us and for those around us.

Often older parents of young adults who no longer go to church are tempted to think that their grown children owe it to them and to their grandchildren to worship with them or practice the Catholic faith. While the desire to include their young adults in their faith or parishes is a God-given desire, a parent can become fixated on this one longing.[44] We admit that this sometimes happens to us. During the baptism of one of our grandchildren, our son-in-law leaned over and whispered to Therese, "Do I have to bring the candle up to the altar?" She was tempted to reply, "Yes—it's the rules!" or "Do you really want your child baptized in the first place?" But through the grace of God, Therese was able to accept this young man and see the situation from his point of view. Her answer was, "It's so you can be the light of her life when she needs it."

We should strive to have the attitude as described by Pope St. John XXIII (1881–1963) in his journal:

> So, I must say very little to anyone about the things that hurt me. Great discretion and forbearance in my judgments of men and situations: willingness to pray particularly for those who may cause me suffering, and in everything great kindness and endless patience, remembering that any other sentiment or mixture of sentiments . . . is contrary to the spirit of the Gospel and of evangelic perfection.[45]

Third: Withhold Judgment and Condemnation

The noblewoman Françoise Blin de Bourdon, who lived during the French Revolution, was told to visit St. Julie Billiart (1751–1816), who could give her counsel about the spiritual life. At first, Françoise was embarrassed when she visited Julie, who had been paralyzed for many years and could not speak clearly. But gradually, Françoise and Julie became co-workers in helping the poor. Later, the two friends became founding members of the Sisters of Notre Dame de Namur. And shortly after, Julie was healed of her paralysis. Françoise is said to have written this: "It is very essential in the spiritual life to have a simple eye; that is, to be ready to accept and to judge favorably all that is not evidently bad."

Françoise's observation raises an important question about patience and forbearance. Aren't we inclined to form judgments and condemn others based on superficial, irritating, or even innocent qualities rather than essential matters? Mother Basilea Schlink, co-founder of the Evangelical Sisterhood of Mary, in her book *Repentance: The Joy-Filled Life*, tells a story about the difficulties of building a new motherhouse: ·

> During the construction the sisters had to push a loader heavily loaded with sand. It was very hard to handle. We were always afraid that if it jumped the track, we could not get it back on again, because most of the sisters did not have the strength to do it. One day it jumped the track six times. Could that be an accident when even a sparrow does not fall to the ground except by God's will?

The sister in charge called everyone to the prayer tent. That is when each of them realized that they had fallen into silently judging one another and blaming each other. So they were reconciled, and the loader did not jump the track after that.[46]

Fourth: Couple Patience with Listening

We talked about listening in the chapter on respect. But how much more crucial listening becomes in a relationship that has difficulties! Listening coupled with patience brings you beyond just keeping your mouth shut and enduring someone's annoying habits.

Early on in our relationship, John would give Therese rides to a weekly faith-sharing group at Holy Cross College along with four other girls. Unfortunately, John was always at least ten minutes late. This was more than annoying for Therese, who puts a high priority on being punctual. So after months of silent aggravation, Therese told John, "If you are on time next week, I will pray for you for the rest of my life." As John tells it, he left the house an hour early in order to arrive exactly on time. When the doorbell rang as the clock struck seven, Therese was shocked and on the verge of berating herself. "Oh no! Why would I make such a foolish promise? How can I pray for someone I don't even like?" So she began to repent of her attitude toward John. And little by little, she began to ask him about his day, about his studies, and about how things were going with his parents. That's when things began to change in the relationship.

Here are some sharing questions that you can ask to get beyond the surface and let go of what you might not like about another person. The goal is an open-ended dialogue.

- Help me understand what you are thinking.

- What gives you the strength to get through this?

- What does this mean for you?

- What is it like for you when . . . ?

After you ask one of these questions, listen attentively for the answer. Then try to repeat what has been said to the satisfaction of the other person. These questions can help dissolve any negative atmosphere and can build a bridge of trust, especially if you can hear the emotions behind what is being said.

It is when we choose patience and listening together that we offer the sacrificial love of Jesus and allow the Word made flesh to dwell among us. Think of Jesus on the cross with two criminals. One lashed out at Jesus. The other defended Jesus and endured his punishment, saying, "Jesus, remember me when you come into your kingdom" (Luke 23:42). What are you tempted to do in a difficult relationship: lash out, run away, or practice listening forbearance?

Fifth: Pray for Self-Control, a Gift of the Spirit

St. Catherine of Siena (1347–1380) wrote, "When it seems that God shows us the faults of others, keep on the safe side—it may be that judgment is false. On your lips let silence abide. . . . If the vice really exists in a person, he will correct himself better, seeing himself so gently understood."[47]

St. Catherine's advice points toward the inner reality that is involved when we think someone is at fault through their words or actions, or even when they possess some unexplained quality that we just don't like. She reminds us that we may be mistaken in our conclusions, or our thinking may be clouded by pride, hatred, cultural background, or prejudice. We once assisted a rough-and-tumble inner-city woman in becoming Catholic. She was so grateful that she told her friends that the Catholic Church was the "best [expletive!] place in the world!" Even though we were embarrassed and annoyed, it was not our place to correct her use of language immediately.

> The fruit of the Spirit is love, joy, peace, patience, kindness, generosity, faithfulness, gentleness, and self-control. There is no law against such things. And those who belong to Christ Jesus have crucified the flesh with its passions and desires. If we live by the Spirit, let us also be guided by the Spirit. (Galatians 5:22-25)

Both St. Catherine's advice and St. Paul's guidance can be seen as explanations of how the gifts of patience and self-control work together. But knowing what to do in a difficult relationship and being able to follow their guidance are often two different realities. This is why we need to turn to the Holy Spirit in prayer over and over again. This is why an important hallmark of the Christian life is relying on the Holy Spirit at every moment in our daily lives.

Once we tried to explain the Holy Spirit to our twelve-year-old daughter Rose, to no avail. Then, since Rose was a singer, John decided to explain the Holy Spirit as the breath of God. "Oh!" she exclaimed with excitement. "I get it! You fill yourself up with as much of God as you can hold. Then you let him go slowly, very slowly, so that he can carry you all the way to the end." Each of us needs to inhale the Spirit of Jesus often. Then we can function with the breath of the Spirit in every situation and relationship in our lives. Gifts of self-control, right judgment, and discernment will follow, and all the fruits of our baptism will blossom.

We can say this prayer with St. John Gabriel Perboyre (1802–1840): "Oh, my Divine Savior, transform me into yourself. . . . May my tongue be the tongue of Jesus. Grant that every faculty of my body may serve only to glorify you. Grant that I may live but in you and by you and for you. That I may say with St. Paul: 'I live now, not I, but Christ lives in me.'"[48]

Reflection Questions

1. What inspires you about the way Jesus related to his disciples? When has someone treated you in the same way? How could you grow in imitating this quality in Jesus?

2. Which of these gifts do you desire in your life today: meekness, patience, humility, forbearance, or self-control? How have you experienced the help of the Holy Spirit in surrendering to one of these gifts?

3. What qualities do you look for in a person? When have you changed your mind about someone's character? How did it happen? How might God have been involved in this relationship?

4. What one piece of guidance in this chapter about relating to difficult people is most helpful? How might this insight apply to mending a relationship? What is least helpful? Why?

Skills for Growing in Patience and Forbearance

Ever given unsolicited advice? Ever made a derogatory remark about someone behind his or her back? Ever condemn someone on the spot? How easy it is to do such things, and how difficult to heed the words of James 1:26: "If any think they are religious, and do not bridle their tongues but deceive their hearts, their religion is worthless."

Here's an exercise for assessing the gift of forbearance in your life.

Step One: *Place an "X" on the line indicating where your behavior has usually fallen when you are irritated. Are you in the middle, or near one side or the other?*

Quick to boil _____Slow to boil

Tell it like it is _____Bite my tongue

Hit the ceiling _____Count to ten

Rant and rave _____Stop and pray

Step Two: *Complete the following prayer, which will help you in the future when you face the temptation to become impatient. Add a behavior, followed by what you think God's response would be.*

Jesus, help me when _____ .
God's Response _____ .

Jesus, help me when _____ .
God's Response:_____ .

Close with this prayer:

Lord, I surrender myself into your arms. Be my spiritual GPS. May your voice direct my every step and emotion on the journey homeward. Jesus, may your presence be the map that I use to find my place today and to understand where I am going. Holy and blessed Spirit, be the compass that I rely on to move forward through this day. Amen.

CHAPTER SEVEN

TRUTH AND HONESTY

Forty years old and pregnant with baby number five—what a shock! Therese decided to call Aunt Lillie for some sympathy. After all, Lillie had also given birth to a child at the age of forty. They spoke for quite a while. Therese felt consoled by Aunt Lillie's careful listening and the stories she had to share. But Therese still had a sense of impending doom. Would previous bouts of gestational diabetes be repeated on a more serious level? What would it be like to start all over again with diapers and sleepless nights? How would she juggle her job with the demands of a new baby? Aunt Lillie picked up on these anxieties and ended their conversation with a very pointed invitation. "Therese," she said, "you have a very important decision to make. Is this good news or bad news? As for me, I have already decided. This is good news!"

On this occasion, as well as on many others, Aunt Lillie was just like Jesus and so many of the saints. She loved Therese just as she was, but she also loved her too much to leave her stuck in turmoil. How many people have you known who were both good listeners and capable of an honest challenge when you needed one? Perhaps it was a teacher, a grandparent, a spouse, or a spiritual director. Perhaps it was Jesus himself, who spoke the truth to you as you read the Scriptures. How do you respond when someone challenges you with the truth? What is it like for you to be honest with others?

Jesus Speaks the Truth

"And the Word became flesh and lived among us, and we have seen his glory, the glory as of a father's only son, full of grace and truth. . . . From his fullness we have all received, grace upon grace" (John 1:14, 16).

As we reflect on the role that grace, coupled with truth, played in Jesus' life, we begin with the prologue to John's Gospel. Jesus is the truth. Jesus breathes, speaks, and embodies the great truth of God's love, redemption, and sanctification. This means that Jesus is meant to be the foundation and the context for everything we say as Christians. Here is an example of Jesus speaking with grace and truth.

> Then Jesus went with them to a place called Gethsemane. . . . Then he said to them, "I am deeply grieved, even to death; remain here, and stay awake with me." And going a little farther, he threw himself on the ground and prayed. . . . Then he came to the disciples and found them sleeping; and he said to Peter, "So, could you not stay awake with me one hour?" (Matthew 26:36, 38-40)

Jesus needed the companionship and comfort of his best friends, and they failed him. But even in this most serious situation, he did not offer them a tongue-lashing. He did not condemn them. But neither did he ignore what they had done. Jesus chose to ask a question. He called them back to his earlier request and to the demands of their friendship.

On this occasion and on many others, it was very common for Jesus to use questions as a way of challenging people. He questioned the Pharisees and scribes during their many encounters. He questioned people in need of healing, like the blind man on the road to Jericho (Luke 18:35-43). He asked challenging questions of his listeners, such as the rich young man (Mark 10:17-31) or the disciples who heard him talk about eating his flesh. "Do you also wish to go away?" he asked them (John 6:67).

Another example involves the Samaritan woman at the well (John 4:1-42). First, Jesus carefully built a relationship of respect with the woman. He kindly asked her for a drink. Jesus did not ignore her because she was a woman. He did not condemn her as a Samaritan. Instead, they shared about the water and the well. Then Jesus spoke about "a spring of water gushing up to eternal life" (verse 14), and the woman was very interested. It was only at this point that he challenged her: "Go, call your husband, and come back" (verse 16). The woman explained that she had no husband, allowing Jesus to deepen the challenge he had for her. Then Jesus could speak about "true worshipers" (verse 23) and himself as the Messiah. She was so convinced of the truth of what he was saying that she hurried off to witness to the whole village—to the same villagers that she had been avoiding.

Surrendering to God's Truth

Each of us can be preoccupied with our own version of the truth. It is only when we choose Jesus as the ultimate way, the greatest truth, and the center of all life that we can truly die to ourselves in our thoughts, in our conversations, and in the "instant replay" that happens in our minds when we feel offended. And it is only in Jesus that we can learn about our true selves.

At one point in our marriage, when we had two toddlers under the age of three, we decided that it was time to welcome a third child into the family. But early in her pregnancy, Therese started questioning the goodness of that decision. She was sick and exhausted, and her mother was seriously ill. John knew he had to do something. He tried helping around the house, but that didn't seem to matter; neither did talking things out. He thought of suggesting a call to the doctor, but she had just seen him.

What to do? Then John realized that Therese would experience peace only by talking to Jesus. So each day when he got home from work, he asked her, "Did you have a chance to pray yet?" The usual answer was, "No, and I don't want to!" But he was convinced that God could help her, so every day he would ask again. About ten days into his campaign, when he again asked, "Therese, did you . . . ?" she cut him off and ran into the bathroom. She knew it would be easier to face God than to face John!

Therese sat on the edge of the tub and cried. She told God about all the diapers, the disturbing visits to Mom, the children's short naps, the nausea. "Right now, I don't need one more obligation. I don't need to pray. I don't want to! I just need to relax. I need to have some fun in my life! Sorry, God, but you're not much fun to talk to." Then she took a deep breath and closed her eyes so that she could listen to God. "Well, Therese, right now you're not much fun either!" That was the breakthrough she needed. God's challenge and sense of humor would keep her going for the next seven months, during which her mother would pass away.

God's Invitation to Grace-Filled, Truthful Conversations

How do you connect Jesus and the often-messy details of your daily life? What does it take to become so "preoccupied" with Jesus, who is "the way, and the truth, and the life" (John 14:6), that you speak of Jesus in word and in deed? We suggest that grace-filled, truthful conversations fall into three categories: (1) affirming speech (as covered in a chapter 5); (2) challenging speech; and (3) faith-sharing conversations. Here are some guidelines for all three types of conversations.

First: Speak out of Compassion and Gentleness

Do you agonize about what to say in a difficult relationship or do you just blurt out what's on your mind? It is good to know where you stand in terms of these two approaches to conversation. Both approaches are meant to be coupled with grace and compassion, but in different ways. The more introverted person who is hesitant to speak most often needs the courage to point out a problem. And the more extroverted person who is apt to speak too quickly needs to stop and first think about another's needs.

An additional way to describe our universal call to compassionate speech is found in St. Paul's Letter to the Ephesians. Paul reminds us that we are one in the unity of the Spirit, not enemies or adversaries, not "children, tossed to and fro" (4:14), but parts of the same body. He exhorts us this way: "Speaking the truth in love, we must grow up in every way into him who is the head, into Christ" (4:15). Paul reminds us that we are called to embrace truth and love together. This exhortation is both the basis for affirming one another with statements about someone's basic goodness and also the foundation for sharing our faith in Jesus. And finally, the call to share the truth with love is the basis for shedding light on the faults and irritating foibles that we face in one another. The Holy Spirit challenges us to combine the truth about a problem with God's love in a way that mends and strengthens relationships instead of destroying them.

Remember, facing all interpersonal difficulties begins with regular prayer for the person, lest you err on the side of disconnecting him or her from God. A change in attitude might also be in order. Review this principle: every fault or weakness is actually the flip side of a good gift. For example, excessive stubbornness is the raw side of perseverance. Being too quick to judge is the negative side of being able to critically analyze situations.

In our own lives, we had the opportunity to confront a family member who had become an alcoholic. Our goal was to share the truth we had observed with firmness and gentleness. Four of us related behaviors we had observed. One said, "I notice that you have fallen down the stairs three times in the past two months." Another said, "I know that you are an exceptional driver, but your car has scrapes on almost every side." We made sure to finish our conversation with these words: "I love you. We love you. And we know that you can overcome whatever is at the bottom of all of this behavior." It was not easy for us to share these observations and affirmations, but it was very important to do so in the loving presence and strength of God's Holy Spirit.

Second: Can Your Relationship Sustain Honest Challenges?

Christ's encounter with the Samaritan woman is a fine example of tending to a relationship before challenging someone. Ask yourself these questions before speaking: Is there an obstacle in my own attitude toward this person that requires forgiveness or repentance before I can speak the truth? Is this a sound relationship? Are we both comfortable with each other? Is this an ongoing relationship that gives us the time we might need to recover after any "damage" is done? Is this person emotionally healthy enough to hear such things right now or at all?

Remember that while you are responsible for acting and speaking in love, you are not responsible for another person's emotions or response to a challenge. Blessed Teresa of Calcutta noted, "Jesus said, 'I am the truth,' and it is your duty and mine to speak the truth. Then it is up to the person who hears it whether to accept or reject it."[49] In the case of our confrontation with an alcoholic family member, it took months and some bad news from the doctor before our loved one began treatment for his illness. All we could do was to continue praying and then talk with him about what the doctor had said.

When you have discerned that a challenge is in order, you can couple your challenge with an affirmation of love and affection. One priest we know offered this advice of what to say in such situations: "I got very agitated and angry when you left me waiting in subzero temperatures in the parking lot, and I love you!" Another person suggests that married couples hold hands while they confront one another. Whatever your style might be, we are sure that Jesus will help you when it is time to speak the truth with gentleness and love in a sound relationship. And remember, even when you must discuss a serious situation, all the gifts, fruits, and charisms of the Holy Spirit are at your disposal: peace, wisdom, faith, healing, understanding, counsel, love, kindness, and gentleness, among others. Pray about which ones you might need first as you speak and what gifts the other person might need in order to listen.

The Scriptures remind us of an additional resource that we might not rely upon as much as we could: the love of the brethren. Many of the New Testament letters and epistles exhort us to love all fellow believers with genuine affection. (Romans 12:10, 1 Thessalonians 4:9, 1 Peter 1:22, and Hebrews 10:24 are good examples.) This means that God gives us a unity between believers that is grounded in Baptism, Confirmation, and the Eucharist. You can rely on this gift. When you have serious difficulties with a relationship, you can rely on the body of Christ through the Sacrament of Reconciliation, spiritual direction, a small faith-group sharing, or a simple conversation with a Christian friend. But remember, when sharing in a small group or one-on-one, talk about your difficulty and feelings without naming the person involved (since this would be more like gossip). Ask for help for yourself as well.

Third: Whose Truth Is It Anyway?

Before you share what you see as an important but difficult truth with someone, it is important to review the beliefs, values, and attitudes that you share (or don't share) with that person. This is because the values you hold in common can become the foundation for moving forward in the relationship. What you hold in common also gives more credence to what you share. You might even state one of these beliefs at the beginning of the conversation. For example, "I think we both share the desire to have peace in our family" or "I believe we both want the best for Aunt Myrtle right now" or "I think we share the desire to see this project be successful." Then pause and listen to whether what you stated is true for the other person.

It is also important to recognize that a certain amount of relativism in our culture can erode our ability to share the truth across generations. You may be speaking with someone who believes that any position or "truth" is as good as any other "truth." A 2007 document on evangelization by the Congregation for the Doctrine of the Faith explains the situation in this way:

> Today . . . with ever-increasing frequency, questions are being raised about the legitimacy of presenting to others . . . that which is held to be true for oneself. Often this is seen as an infringement of other people's freedom. Such a vision of human freedom, . . . "recognizing nothing as definitive, leaves as the ultimate criterion only the self with its desires and under the semblance of freedom, becomes a prison for each one" (Pope Benedict).[50]

This kind of thinking can make it more difficult to challenge another person, but as long as the grace of God is at work in a relationship, it is not impossible to overcome.

We learned about seeking the truth in the midst of conflicting values when we sought assistance for our daughter Rose, who had an unusual learning disability. Even though we had supporting test results, Rose was denied any help by the special education committee at her elementary school. We were beyond frustrated—we were heartbroken. So John approached the school psychologist about our options, and together they came up with a plan to appeal the decision. The key would be for one of us to share our observations of Rose when she was trying to do homework. So off we went on the feast of St. Frances Cabrini (1850–1917), encouraged by the prayerful aid of this tiny woman who would scold construction workers twice her size.

At the meeting, one professional after another stated reasons why Rose didn't need help. The most popular reason was her extraordinary intelligence. Then the school psychologist turned to Therese and said, "Would you share your reasons for this appeal?" Therese responded, "Every day she sits at her desk, and after an hour, with less than a fourth of her homework done, she starts to cry. So I go to her and put my arm around her. 'Why am I so stupid, Mom?' she asks me." Every teacher in the room was visibly moved by this story. Silence followed. Then the head of the committee said, "She's approved for resource-room assistance."

Fourth: Respect a Person's Spiritual Needs

No matter what the challenge you must share with someone, there is often an underlying spiritual need that is a part of another person's behavior. So there may be times when the loving thing to do is to pay attention to the underlying spiritual dimension of a person's life. This is when faith sharing comes into the picture. Here is an example of a time when Therese was able to share an experience of faith with her dad.

Dad was scheduled to leave the hospital for a nursing home after surgery to amputate his sole remaining leg. His kidneys had already begun to fail, and he was barely able to speak. Therese joined her siblings at the hospital. When it came time for most of them to leave, Therese suggested that they sing because Dad was a choir member from way back, and he loved to sing.

"What would we sing?" her brother asked. But before anyone could respond, Dad sat bolt upright and said, "Whatever!" We were shocked, too shocked to follow through on the idea.

Therese lingered behind. As they waited for the ambulance to arrive, she wanted to offer some spiritual comfort. Therese decided to sing old and new hymns to him while they held hands. At the end of one song, he said, "Our Father, Our Father," so they prayed a decade of the rosary. At another point, Therese found herself singing "The Holy Ghost Will Set Your Feet to Dancing"— to a guy with no legs! Right before the ambulance came, he said, "Thank you, Therese. I love you." Dad died the next morning at 5:20. And even though he couldn't say much, Therese and her dad had ventured into both faith sharing and evangelizing.

Here is a definition, taken from the U.S. bishops' document *Go and Make Disciples,* for what begins to happen in these spiritual conversations:

> Evangelizing means bringing the Good News of Jesus into every human situation and seeking to convert individuals and society by the divine power of the Gospel itself. At its essence are the proclamation of salvation in Jesus Christ and the response of a person in faith, which are both works of the Spirit of God.[51]

This means that when we address the spiritual needs of others, we do so expecting the Holy Spirit to bless the person with whom we are sharing. Our confidence in the Holy Spirit creates peace in us, no matter what the person's response is. We can even let the other person lead the conversation after we have shared what we have to say. We are also free to give the person as much time as he or she needs after the conversation to think about what was shared.

It is through our courage to enter into this kind of spiritual sharing that many will experience the gospel of Jesus Christ as truly good news for them. In her Catholic best-seller *Forming Intentional Disciples: The Path to Knowing and Following Jesus*, Sherry Weddell describes the five thresholds of conversion that someone needs to cross in order to become a committed disciple of Jesus Christ: initial trust, spiritual curiosity, spiritual openness, spiritual seeking, and intentional discipleship.[52] Learning how to love others as Christ does is the foundation for helping others cross these thresholds in conversation. Our goal as intentional evangelizers is to become the kind of disciple who can recognize the Holy Spirit working in the life of an inactive Catholic or an unchurched person and then have the grace to speak about the greatest truth of all.

Fifth: Pointers for Speaking the Truth in Love

We hope to summarize what has been said in this chapter by offering a set of guidelines for honesty and for sharing the truth in love. We are confident that as you grow in being a disciple of Jesus, he will guide you to an even greater clarity than what we offer here.

1. Speak with gentleness and confidence in God's love for the person whom you address. This does not mean that difficult feelings won't emerge. It does means that your goal is another's wholeness. You are not adversaries but brothers and sisters in our Lord and Savior Jesus Christ.

2. Try presenting the truth of the matter through a question. "Have you ever thought of . . . ?" "What would happen if . . . ?" "What have you tried so far?" "What are you options when . . . ?" Then listen carefully for the other person's point of view and needs.

3. Report your own observations about another's behavior using "I" statements: "I noticed that you . . . " or "I felt . . . when you . . . " Remember the way Jesus spoke to his disciples in the Garden of Gethsemane. It takes humility to approach another this way, especially if you have been trained to assign blame for hurt.

4. Admit that you may not be the right person to share what needs to be said in a serious situation. If that is the case, then turn to someone who may be able to help you sort out your options in the relationship, or who can offer some kind of intervention when a third person would be helpful. And finally, realize that there are times when it is necessary to walk away from a relationship on a permanent basis.

5. Consider the quality of your relationship and the importance of the matter at hand. Is this person a parent? A spouse? A

friend? An employee? Ask if the matter is serious enough for a challenge. We are called to honesty in all things unless the role we have in a relationship, or the topic, makes it inappropriate to speak. When in doubt, ask permission to share a difficulty you are having.

6. Try making an agreement about challenging behavior. For example, Mark and Barbara were in the habit of criticizing the Sunday sermon after Mass on the way to the coffee shop. Mark realized how inappropriate and unkind this was. So he asked Barbara, "Next time I start complaining, would you please say, 'Mark, you told me you didn't want to do this anymore'?"

7. Never challenge a person in front of others. Do so privately in order to protect that person's dignity. Once when John was visiting his Uncle Arthur, who was in a coma, Arthur's brother Ned was also visiting. Ned began to talk about how awful Arthur looked and how soon he would die. Then Arthur began to twitch and tried to raise his hand. So John asked to speak to Ned in the hallway. He explained that Arthur might be able to hear him and that it might be upsetting him. When they returned to the room, they spoke softly to Arthur and prayed a Hail Mary with him. Then the twitching stopped.

Reflection Questions

1. Jesus referred to himself as "the way, and the truth, and the life" (John 14:6). What does this mean for you? What steps could you take to accept Jesus as the most important truth in your daily life?

2. How has someone spoken the truth in love when you needed guidance? How did you respond? When have you challenged someone with the truth? How were you received?

3. What was your experience of conflict as a child? How has this experience carried into adulthood? Which kind of relationship is most troublesome for you: parent and child, boss and worker, husband and wife, or friends in a social group?

4. Which of the suggestions in the fifth section, "Pointers for Speaking the Truth in Love," is easiest for you to put into practice? Which is most difficult? Why?

Skills for Growing in the Truth

In the Gospels, it is common for Jesus' followers to have difficulty accepting the truth about who Jesus is and what he came to do for us. Their responses demonstrate varying levels of confusion, and sometimes they even seem in denial about what Jesus has taught them. Here are some examples.

1. After the healing of the woman with a hemorrhage, Jesus asked, "Who touched my clothes?" (Mark 5:30). The disciples didn't seem to understand Jesus' capacity to heal when they responded, "You see the crowd pressing in on you; how can you say, 'Who touched me?'" (5:31).

2. After the death of Lazarus, Mary, his sister, came out to meet Jesus with a lack of confidence in his desire to save and said, "Lord, if you had been here, my brother would not have died" (John 11:32).

3. When the mother of two disciples approached Jesus, she said, "Declare that these two sons of mine will sit, one at your right hand and one at your left, in your kingdom" (Matthew 20:21). She misunderstood his mission and could not see Jesus as anything more than an earthly ruler.

Which example parallels some of your reactions and confusion about what God is doing in your life? Recall a time when you were confused or prone to blame, or you made unrealistic demands of God. Did you misunderstand Jesus' capacity and desire (1) to heal, (2) to save us, or (3) to share his mission with us? Find a quiet place and talk to Jesus about this situation. Tell him how you feel, and think about what his response might be.

Close with this prayer:

Lord Jesus, I want to give you my thoughts, especially when I become narrow-minded.

Lord Jesus, help me surrender the faulty conclusions about you and about others that I embrace so easily and so often.

Send your Spirit of light and truth.
Send your Spirit of humility and peace.
Send your Spirit of wisdom and patience.
Send your Spirit of hope and love.

I want to rely on your most holy Counselor when I open my mouth to speak. I want to be an instrument of your words and love always. Amen.

CHAPTER EIGHT

HEALING PRESENCE

As parish director of religious education, John's office was somewhat hidden away in the church basement, but catechists with serious problems found him anyway. This time it was by phone. His heart skipped a beat when he heard Barbara's pain-filled voice. The next night she and her physician husband were to teach a session on sexuality for seventy teenage Confirmation candidates.

"John, I threw out my back, so we have to cancel for tomorrow night. I'm so sorry." Barbara had injured a disc in her back and expected to be bedridden for two weeks or more. John asked if Barbara's husband was there to help her with their young children. He was. Then John said, "Barbara, I believe that Jesus wants to help us when we are suffering. Can we pray an Our Father together for the Holy Spirit to be with you and to help you?" After praying together, they hung up.

The next morning John received a second call from Barbara. "John! I felt something like heat moving up and down my back while we were praying on the phone and afterward. Then I went to bed for the night. When I woke up, *all* the pain was gone. I can move freely! Alleluia! And my husband Al is sitting in the living room crying for joy." That night Barbara and Al began their talk by witnessing about her physical healing. Then they continued to share about the healing presence of Jesus Christ in their married sexual relationship.

When have you suffered and needed God's touch? How have you brought your suffering to Jesus? What happened? How was he with you in your pain?

Jesus Offers a Healing Presence

One of the most interesting healing stories in the Gospels involved an everyday kind of a miracle. "When Jesus entered Peter's house, he saw his mother-in-law lying in bed with a fever; he touched her hand, and the fever left her, and she got up and began to serve him" (Matthew 8:14-15). This healing flowed from the disciples' day-to-day friendship with Jesus. It is not unlike the raising of Lazarus from the dead that was based on the friendship between Lazarus, Mary, Martha, and Jesus.

A second healing involved a widow's only son who had died and was being carried out of the city of Nain (Luke 7:11-17). This healing happened while Jesus was passing by. But there was nothing accidental or haphazard about Jesus' compassion. Luke tells us that there was no one else to care for this widow—she was about to become a beggar in the streets. Perhaps Jesus was moved by the thought of what might happen to his own mother as controversy with the Jewish leaders took its normal course. "When the Lord saw her, he had compassion for her and said to her, 'Do not weep.' . . . And he said, 'Young man, I say to you, rise!' . . . and Jesus gave him to his mother" (7:13-15). Both were touched by God.

But Jesus did not just perform all the healings on his own. Later on, Jesus treated his disciples as apprentices, showing them how to pray, teach, and heal. He sent them out to be a part of his healing love for the world as evangelizing missionaries, proclaiming the good news of God's loving compassion (Luke 10:1-12). The Scriptures tell us that he "rejoiced" (*agalliao*) when they returned and shared all that God had done through them (10:21). Given that *agalliao* means to "exult" or to "rejoice exceedingly," we could say that Jesus jumped for joy!

Surrendering to God's Healing Presence

Returning to our opening story, John struggled with his response to Barbara's pain. Anxiety and concerns about himself flooded his mind as he listened to Barbara's story about her injured back. "How will I cover that teenage Confirmation class tomorrow?" At first, John was tempted to distance himself from Barbara's problem. Then Jesus helped him catch himself in mid-worry, filling him with compassion for what Barbara and her husband were going through. Instead of hanging up immediately to study the material, he offered to pray with her to the Holy Spirit. His greatest desire became connecting Barbara to Jesus.

In prayer, John gave the Holy Spirit permission to do whatever was needed to help Barbara with her pain and assist her family. His experience was akin to this image, from Blessed Teresa of Calcutta, of the grace of the Holy Spirit:

When you look at the inner workings of electrical things, you often see small and big wires, new and old, cheap and expensive, all lined up. Until the current passes through them there will be no light.

The wire is you and me. The current is God. We have the power to let the current pass through us, use us, and produce the light of the world. Or we can refuse to be used and allow darkness to spread.[53]

John knew that Jesus had promised to be present (Matthew 28:20) and that he himself was not the healer, just the wire. And today we are just as confident that Jesus will be with you also as you reach out to others. Jesus has already given you the power to live this healing presence through the sacraments. The Father has promised to heal you and release an ocean of Jesus' compassion for you. The Holy Spirit has promised to transform you so that you can echo his healing presence to others, even when no words are spoken. And finally, you are not alone. God energizes us together as parishes. You are part of a whole body on fire with Jesus. As Pope Francis has reminded us,

> An evangelizing community gets involved by word and deed in people's daily lives; it bridges distances, it is willing to abase itself if necessary, and it embraces human life, touching the suffering flesh of Christ in others. Evangelizers thus take on the "smell of the sheep" and the sheep are willing to hear their voice.[54]

God's Invitation to Be a Healing Presence

Jesus invites you to be his follower and to become his compassionate, healing presence for others in your day-to-day life. God calls you to watch for another person's pain and pressing needs. Jesus invites you to be his disciple for the sake of the people who are literally dying to know the healing love of God. Jesus said, "The harvest is plentiful, but the laborers are few; therefore ask the Lord of the harvest to send out laborers into his harvest" (Matthew 9:37-38).

Before you take any of the following steps, it is important to allow Jesus to be present to you through daily prayer (at least fifteen to twenty minutes a day). Then you are more likely to be a healing presence of God to others. When you don't pray, you become blind to the needs of others and insensitive to the Holy Spirit's leadings in your heart. Why not stop now and pray this prayer of St. Augustine (354–430)?

Breathe into me, Holy Spirit, that my thoughts may all be holy.
Move in me, Holy Spirit, that my work, too, may be holy.
Attract my heart, Holy Spirit, that I may love only what is holy.
Strengthen me, Holy Spirit, that I may defend all that is holy.
Protect me, Holy Spirit, that I may always be holy.[55]

First: Be Fully Present to Each Person

In the Acts of the Apostles, St. Luke points out stepping-stones for journeying with others who need the healing presence of God. "When [the lame man] saw Peter and John about to go into the temple, he asked them for alms. Peter looked intently at him, as did John, and said, 'Look at us.' And he fixed his attention on them, expecting to receive something from them" (3:3-5). Look at each person in your day with new eyes—with respect (see chapter 2). Listen with one ear to the person's needs, stresses, and infirmities, and with the other ear, listen to the Holy Spirit's desire to bless and abide with this person.

Bianca was a college professor who went through a deep conversion to Christ after surviving a serious car accident. She realized just how precious life is and how precious each person is to Jesus. Bianca vowed from then on to build time into her daily schedule for one-on-one conversations with students who came to her. Either she would give that student five minutes immediately or set up an appointment for a conversation later. When Bianca spoke about her decision to love others in this way during a talk on a weekend retreat, Craig experienced a new conversion to Jesus. At the end of the weekend, Craig went up to Bianca to thank her for sharing her story. He then turned to walk away but stopped and explained, "Because of your witness to Jesus, I can never again turn my back on other people."

As the Second Vatican Council reminds us in the opening of the document *Gaudium et Spes*, "The joys and the hopes, the griefs and the anxieties of the men of this age, especially those who are poor or in any way afflicted, these are the joys and hopes, the griefs and anxieties of the followers of Christ. Indeed, nothing genuinely human fails to raise an echo in their hearts."[56]

Second: Practice the Daily "Art of Accompaniment"

Surrender yourself to the Spirit in prayer every day. The power to love your neighbor and yourself flows from the Spirit. That Spirit is the very love of God that the Father and the Son have for us. We are like poor buckets or vases that are filled with the Spirit, but because of our sins, we leak! We lose track of God's presence. So the more we turn to the Holy Spirit, the more our sins are washed away and the more capable we become of loving beyond our human strength, loving even those whom we call or who call us "the enemy."

Remember, returning to our story from Acts, Peter and John were on their way to pray in the Temple. Being on the way to pray is, in fact, praying. When they met the lame man, they did not toss a few good wishes or good advice at him. They befriended him and allowed the Holy Spirit to reach out to him from the depths of their beings where the love of God resided. "But Peter said, 'I have no silver or gold, but what I have I give you; in the name of Jesus Christ of Nazareth, stand up and walk.' And he took him by the right hand and raised him up" (3:6-7). They asked Jesus to heal the man and then grasped his hand as a member of God's family, a brother in the Lord.

Pope Francis calls this way of being present to others the "art of accompaniment."

> This "art of accompaniment" . . . teaches us to remove our sandals before the sacred ground of the other (cf. Exodus 3:5). The pace of this accompaniment must be steady and reassuring, reflecting our closeness and our compassionate gaze which also heals, liberates and encourages growth in the Christian life.[57]

Third: Trust Jesus to Heal You and Others in His Own Way

Like so many others, you may be tempted to dictate the kind of healing you want and how it should happen. You may be tempted to tell God what to do and to expect Jesus to heal you and your loved ones instantly. But this is not how God usually works. Instead, you are called to the total surrender of your whole life to Jesus, who is the way. When you do this, you can trust that Jesus will heal you, not necessarily in the manner that you want, but rather in the way that you most need it. Think of the army commander from the Old Testament, Naaman, who asked Elisha to heal him of leprosy but became angry when the prophet told him to wash seven times in the Jordan River. It took several servants to convince him to obey; then he was healed (2 Kings 5:1-19). It seems that God was as interested in his conversion as his healing.

You may be tempted to ask for God's healing and help only once, and then stop. You may be tempted to think you aren't worthy because you have failed at loving others. But you can still turn your life over to Christ, and he will heal you. In the Gospels, it is those who have taken wrong turns and have recognized their mistakes that are more open to Jesus' healing message.

What about people who are not healed when we pray? Therese's mother, Claire, had two back-to-back surgeries for ulcerative colitis. She was dangerously ill. People in our faith community took turns praying around the clock for several days, but the infection kept spreading throughout her body. Therese remembers visiting Mom on a Tuesday night. Her arms were cold, the readings on the monitors did not look good, and she was near death. So Therese told Mom that she would go to church and pray with everyone who had gathered there that evening. When she arrived at the church, a friend named Kevin told Therese about a vision he had of her mom. Kevin described all the monitors exactly as Therese had seen them. "Then Jesus walked into Claire's room with a white lab coat on. Claire sat up and smiled. 'You will be okay now, Claire. Come with me,' he said. And they left the room together." Mom died a few minutes later.

We have learned that all healing that happens in this life—whether physical, emotional, or spiritual—is only partial. One day we must all surrender to the complete healing that happens when we die and go to be with the Lord Jesus in heaven with all the angels and saints. Claire was given a complete healing. Since then, her witness to Christ in life and in death has inspired many to seek a deeper relationship with Jesus and with the Church. And our own suffering at losing her has empowered us to walk with others who are wounded (2 Corinthians 1:3-7).

Fourth: Offer to Pray with a Person in the Present Moment

Pope Francis reminds us that since others have helped us experience the healing presence of Jesus, we, in turn, are now empowered to bring others to Jesus. "Someone good at such accompaniment does not give in to frustrations or fears. He or she invites others to let themselves be healed, to take up their mat, embrace the cross, leave all behind and go forth ever anew to proclaim the Gospel."[58]

If you have never tried to pray with another person, here are five steps that will guide you:

1. Know that Jesus is with both of you. Invite the person to imagine and focus on a favorite image or statue of Jesus. You might also begin with Psalm 23. Give the person the option of closing his or her eyes. You might acknowledge the presence of Jesus with words like "Thank you, Jesus" or "I know you are with us now."

2. Pray specifically for the person's request: "Help me, Jesus, with
. . . " or "Help my brother or sister with . . . " Pray also for the
"core" needs that lie beneath what the person has expressed.
Say things like "God, we give you everything that contrib-
utes to this situation" or "God, we give you any confusion or
depression that Joanne may be feeling" or "God, we give you
Joanne's unspoken pain." If the person has requested prayer
for someone else, first pray for the person in front of you. Then
pray together for the person who is not present.

3. Give the Holy Spirit permission to do whatever is needed: physical, spiritual, or emotional healing; conviction of sin; removal
of obstacles; a new home, job, or attitude; or help finding ways
to deal with failure, suffering, or shame.

4. While praying, watch and listen for the action of the Holy Spirit
in the person (crying, laughter, peace, release of tension, words,
images, and so forth). After two or three minutes, ask the person to describe what has been happening within their hearts
while you prayed. If he or she mentions something specific,
pray for a few more minutes, using their experience as a guide.

5. Thank Jesus for whatever the Holy Spirit is doing, even if you
cannot see anything happening. End your prayer time by inviting the person to repeat after you each line of the prayer below.
Or you might want to pray a traditional prayer aloud, like the
Our Father, the Hail Mary, or the Glory Be.

> Come Holy Spirit, fill the hearts of your faithful
> and kindle in [us] the fire of your love.
> Send forth your Spirit and [we] shall be created.
> And You shall renew the face of the earth.[59]

Fifth: Move Outward to Evangelize Others

God challenges us as individuals and as a Church to be a healing presence in the culture and the world around us. God invites us to enter into the healing presence of Jesus so that the places where we go will become holy places. Then every corner of God's world will be transformed by the particular healing gifts that God gives, whether these gifts involve listening, touch, spending a few extra moments with someone, or a brief prayer.

To continue with the Scripture story about the lame man, "And [Peter] took him by the right hand and raised him up; and immediately his feet and ankles were made strong. Jumping up, he stood and began to walk, and he entered the temple with them, walking and leaping and praising God" (Acts 3:7-8). When people gathered to see what was happening, Peter preached the good news of Jesus Christ to them: "Repent therefore, and turn to God so that your sins may be wiped out, so that times of refreshing may come from the presence of the Lord, and that he may send the Messiah appointed for you, that is, Jesus" (3:19-20). As in the healing of Peter's mother-in-law, there is within this event a deeper call to become Christ's disciples and to evangelize others.

According to Pope Francis,

Genuine spiritual accompaniment always begins and flourishes in the context of service to the mission of evangelization. Paul's relationship with Timothy and Titus provides an example of this accompaniment and formation which takes place in the midst of apostolic activity. . . . Missionary disciples accompany missionary disciples.[60]

After graduating from college, John felt called by Jesus to a life of full-time lay ministry. But he was experiencing severe fatigue. Doctors ran tests and discovered that his thyroid gland had stopped working. Even with medications, he would need ten to twelve hours of rest each day. The conclusion was that his health might make lay ministry impossible. Then a close friend was inspired to give John an all-expenses-paid ticket to a Catholic conference at the University of Notre Dame in Indiana, where there would be a major healing service. During the bus trip to the conference, John came down with a severe case of the flu. After arriving on campus, all he wanted to do was crawl into bed and sleep. Yet crowds of people around him were streaming to a Mass of thanksgiving for a safe arrival. So John decided to join them. When he received the Eucharist, he was healed of the flu instantaneously. And when he got home several days later, he felt so good that his doctors retested him for thyroid disease. They confirmed that he no longer had the disease. John was healed and strengthened so that he could serve as a parish, diocesan, and national lay leader for decades to come.

With St. Paul we pray, "Blessed be the God and Father of our Lord Jesus Christ, the Father of mercies and the God of all consolation, who consoles us in all our affliction, so that we may be able to console those who are in any affliction with the consolation with which we ourselves are consoled by God" (2 Corinthians 1:3-4).

Reflection Questions

1. When have you suffered and needed the Holy Spirit's healing presence and touch?

2. How have you brought your suffering to Jesus? What happened? How were others a sign of God's compassion toward you? How was Jesus there with you in your pain?

3. How can you embrace Jesus Christ's healing presence more fully in your own life today?

4. Whom do you know right now that needs the healing presence of the Holy Spirit? How is Christ's Spirit calling you to be a healing, mending presence to that person and to others in your everyday life?

Skills for Growing in God's Healing Presence

In the events of the Gospels, Jesus is often on the road, whether it is the road that goes around the Sea of Galilee, the road to Jerusalem, or an unnamed highway. Many healings happen while he is on his way somewhere else. So imagine yourself by the side of the road. Find a good place to encounter Jesus amidst the details of the scene.

Step One: *Reflect on the details of where you are waiting. What do you imagine about the sights, sounds, smells, or the weather? How big is the crowd? What are the people like who stand or wait beside you? What kind of help do you need from Jesus? Are you blind, deaf, or lame?*

Step Two: *Read Luke 18:35-43 slowly. Jesus is coming! But it is hard to get to him. You must call out to Jesus in order to be heard. What name for Jesus would you use: Good Shepherd, Savior, Son of David, Lord, or another? Call out to him now, over and over again.*

Step Three: *Read Luke 18:35-43 slowly for a second time, pausing after words, phrases, or images that encourage or challenge you. Now imagine your encounter with Jesus. What does he say and do?*

Step Four: *Thank him for what you experience. What would you do after he touches you? How would your experience change how you treat other needy people by the side of the road?*

Spend a few moments thanking God for the times when you recovered from an illness or were protected by God. Finish by praying a Hail Mary.

Conclusion

On July 17, 1996, just twelve minutes after takeoff, TWA Flight 800 exploded and crashed. The wreckage plunged into the Atlantic Ocean just eight miles off the coast of Center Moriches, New York, on the south shore of Long Island. All 230 people on board were killed.

A helipad had been built at the U.S. Coast Guard Station in East Moriches, and the station became a base for emergency responders as well as a media hub and the site where bodies were received. In the days that followed, more than 5,000 family members, federal investigators, and news reporters descended on that town of only 6,000 residents. Today there are parks at the Smith Point and Center Moriches beaches dedicated to those who died in the crash, with plaques bearing their names.

St. John the Evangelist Parish in Center Moriches was at the heart of this tragedy. Six members of the parish were on the plane when it crashed. The pastor, Fr. Jim, opened the church and school buildings for whatever relief services were needed. He celebrated Mass every day to comfort and guide the workers and the victims' families during this terrible time. Fr. Jim's daily homilies were featured each night on national news broadcasts. He spoke about the cross of Jesus as the only way to make sense of such suffering.

In addition, parishioners stepped forward in large numbers to comfort the suffering and help the investigators and media professionals in any way they could. A few months later, at an evangelistic Ash Wednesday service, parents of a young woman who had died in the crash gave their witness about how Fr. Jim and members of St. John's had given them hope in Jesus Christ during this heart-wrenching crisis. They had been embraced by the body of Christ.

Two years prior to the crash, God had begun to prepare the parish for this intense ministry. We were part of a team of laypeople from the Renewal offices of the Diocese of Rockville Centre that had trained Fr. Jim and hundreds of parishioners to develop a culture of Catholic witness and evangelization at St. John's. As a result, they had decided to use Ash Wednesday and Lent as an annual season of parish-wide evangelization. Within hours after the TWA 800 explosion, Fr. Jim called John on the phone, declaring, "This is the worst of times for our parish! It is one of the most difficult situations I have ever faced. Yet I realized something last night while I was praying that maybe this is one of those 'evangelizing moments' you taught us about. Maybe this is a moment rich with opportunities to evangelize people to Jesus Christ and to him crucified!" John's heart leapt for joy, "Yes, it is!" he said. They stopped and prayed over the phone together for the people of the parish, for the town, for the media, for the families of the victims, and for the workers and visitors who were coming.

When the tragedy of TWA 800 happened around them, Fr. Jim and the people of St. John's were in the midst of learning to love others as Christ does. But they knew that it would be impossible without God's intervention. So together they sought more love and grace from God. They knew that intercession, respect, forgiveness, gratitude, affirmation, forbearance, truth, and healing would be powerful tools for making sense of it all. So together they sought more from God. And together they embodied the exhortation of St. Philip Neri (1515–1595): "Cast yourself into the arms of God and be very sure that if he wants anything of you, he will fit you for the work and give you strength."[61]

We tell this story because the eight pathways in this book are not just callings for individuals but also for whole communities. And it is when whole communities follow these paths in imitation of Jesus that people around us will be inspired and loved in ways that reflect the lived gospel of Jesus Christ. Also, each of the eight ways, and all of them together, converge in the person of Jesus and him crucified. Finally, even though each of them is the "narrow gate" (Matthew 7:13-14) challenging us to die to selfishness and sin as we struggle to forgive others, to thank others, and to be patient with irritating people, God will shower his blessings on us. When we yield to the little "deaths" that the pathways require, we are raised up with Jesus through the person of the Holy Spirit. The Spirit will grant us the gifts and fruits we need in order to love others as Christ does so that we can mend broken relationships and build strong ones.

When we go beyond our limits in loving others, Jesus will love through us. When we realize that we are weak, he will be strong. When we stop seeking our own fulfillment and long for the true and eternal happiness of others, good things will happen.

We saw the fruit of accepting this invitation to die and rise with Christ in our relationship with John's mom, Mary. When we would stay at her home, she would place several large pieces of newspaper on the floor beneath the chairs of our toddlers. Then she would put a full-length bib on each of the children and serve them in bowls with suction cups attached to the bottom so they couldn't throw them. Therese especially agonized over all of these precautions but smiled at Mom and thanked her for her help.

Years later, Therese asked Mary when her love for cleaning had started. She confessed that it was while she was hiding in the closet as a child to get away from her parents who, during their many heated arguments, would throw cups of hot tea at each other. Even when it was safe to come out, there would be tea stains on the walls to remind the frightened child of what had happened. It was during one especially terrifying episode in the closet that little Mary kept repeating to herself, "*My* house will never be dirty! *My* house will never be dirty!" To this day, we are convinced that our feeble attempts to love John's mom while our toddlers ate gave her the freedom to share this story and to experience great inner healing.

God is calling you to try the eight ways of mending and strengthening your relationships so that you will be filled to the brim with a love born of intercession, respect, forgiveness, gratitude, affirmation, forbearance, truth, and a healing presence. You too are called to that death to self—that "surrender" moment, that "power" moment—along each of these pathways to holiness. You too can be transformed by reaching out for Jesus' hand, surrendering to his wisdom, and following him in your daily life through this eightfold mission of healing that will draw others to Christ. And through your attempts to love, you will be connecting others to Jesus. In short, you will become a missionary of the love of God, as Pope Francis explains:

> My mission of being in the heart of the people is not just a part of my life or a badge I can take off; it is not an "extra" or just

another moment in life. Instead, it is something I cannot uproot from my being without destroying my very self. I am a mission on this earth; that is the reason why I am here in this world. We have to regard ourselves as sealed, even branded, by this mission of bringing light, blessing, enlivening, raising up, healing and freeing.[62]

Remember, these eight paths have a single destination, the New Jerusalem of heaven, where we will be surrounded by and immersed in love with all of God's people and all the angels and saints forever. Love is our home. Love is what every human person longs for. Love is the foundation for the process of the New Evangelization. Our love is meant to operate with companion gifts of prayer, sharing faith in conversation, and inviting others to experience Jesus and the body of Christ with us. When we keep this in mind, we are imitating the approach of Jesus and the apostles in Scripture. Jesus prayed often. He offered compassionate care through listening and healings. Jesus shared what he knew about our heavenly Father. He dared to invite many people to faith through parables and questions of all kinds. And finally, he dared many, like the rich young man and the disciples, to follow him together as a community, as the communion of the saints who are heavenbound.

So let us love others with the same confidence that Jesus had through the power of the Holy Spirit. Let us move forward, endowed with the gifts and fruits of the Holy Spirit given in Baptism, Confirmation, and the Eucharist. Let us become the fire of his love for all those around us. "If you are friends with Christ many others will warm themselves at your fire. . . . The day when you no longer burn with love, many will die of the cold."[63] Let us take heart. The Spirit wants to use us as instruments of God's love for others. Learning how will be messy at times, but the task, the mission, and the journey will bring fulfillment and happiness beyond our wildest dreams.

"The Spirit of the Lord is upon me,
    because he has anointed me to bring good news to the poor.
He has sent me to proclaim release to the captives
    and recovery of sight to the blind, to let the oppressed go free,
to proclaim the year of the Lord's favor." (Luke 4:18-19)

Endnotes

1. Jill Haak Adels, *The Wisdom of the Saints: An Anthology* (Oxford, England: Oxford University Press, 1989), 137.

2. *The Collected Works of St. Teresa of Avila, Volume I*, trans. Kieran Kavanaugh, OCD, and Otilio Rodriguez, OCD (Washington, DC: ICS Publications, 1980), 98.

3. Jill Haak Adels, 39.

4. *Register of the Epistles of Saint Gregory the Great*, Book IX, Epistle I, To Januarius, Bishop of Caralis, http://www.documentacatholicaomnia.eu/01p/0590-0604,_SS_Gregorius_I_Magnus,_Registri_Epistolarum_%5BSchaff%5D,_EN.pdf.

5. Francis, *Evangelii Gaudium* [On the Joy of the Gospel], §282-283, http://w2.vatican.va/content/francesco/en/apost_exhortations/documents/papa-francesco_esortazione-ap_20131124_evangelii-gaudium.html.

6. For the purposes of this book, we are limiting our discussion to the gifts of the Holy Spirit (wisdom, understanding, counsel, knowledge, fortitude, piety, and fear of the Lord) and the fruits of the Spirit (love, joy, peace, patience, kindness, goodness, generosity, meekness, faithfulness, modesty, continence, and chastity). But keep in mind that there are also charisms of the Holy Spirit: freely bestowed gifts and graces given for the body of Christ like prophecy, healing, discernment, and speaking in tongues. And all of these phenomena are meant to function together.

7. John Paul II, *Veritatis Splendor* [The Splendor of Truth], §21, http://w2.vatican.va/content/john-paul-ii/en/encyclicals/documents/hf_jp-ii_enc_06081993_veritatis-splendor.html.

8. Benedict XVI, *Deus Caritas Est* [God is Love], §14, http://w2.vatican.va/content/benedict-xvi/en/encyclicals/documents/hf_ben-xvi_enc_20051225_deus-caritas-est.html.

9. Morton T. Kelsey, *The Art of Christian Love* (Pecos, NM: Dove Publications, 1974), 15.

10. Thomas Dubay, SM, *Caring: A Biblical Theology of Community* (Denville, NJ: Dimension Books, 1973), 85.

11. John Paul II, *Christifideles Laici* [The Lay Members of Christ's Faithful People], §40, http://w2.vatican.va/content/john-paul-ii/en/apost_exhortations/documents/hf_jp-ii_exh_30121988_chris-tifideles-laici.html.

12. Francis, *Evangelii Gaudium*, 199.

13. Quentin Hakenewerth, SM, *The Grain of Wheat: Dynamics for Spiritual Growth* (St. Louis, MO: The North American Center for Marianist Studies, 1997), 6.

14. Paul VI, *Evangelii Nuntiandi* [On Evangelization in the Modern World], 52, http://w2.vatican.va/content/paul-vi/en/apost_exhor-tations/documents/hf_p-vi_exh_19751208_evangelii-nuntiandi.html.

15. "A Big Heart Open to God: The exclusive interview with Pope Francis," by Antonio Spadaro, SJ, *America*, September 30, 2013, http://www.americamagazine.org/pope-interview.

16. John of the Cross, *John of the Cross: Selected Writings (Classics of Western Spirituality)*, ed. Kieran Kavanaugh, OCD (Mahwah, NJ: Paulist Press, 1988), 293–294, stanzas 1, 3–4.

17. Therese Boucher, "Come Holy Spirit," *YouTube* video, 3:12, July 12, 2007, http://www.youtube.com/watch?v=B7FHcVCGO-A.

18. John Vianney, qtd. in "Reflections: Our Father's Love: The Mercy of God," MyCatholicSource.com, http://www.mycatholicsource .com/mcs/qt/our_fathers_love_reflections_mercy_of_God.htm.

19. Francis de Sales, qtd. in "Trust and Mercy: Reflections on Divine Mercy Sunday," BiblicalCatholic.com, http://www.biblicalcath-olic.com/apologetics/s22.htm.

20. Antonio Spadaro, SJ.

21. "The Father Wound Epidemic: Interview with Dr. Richard Fitz-gibbons" by Fathers for Good, http://www.fathersforgood.org/ ffg/en/month/archive/march10.html, and H. Norman Wright, *Healing for the Father Wound: A Trusted Christian Counselor Offers Time-Tested Advice* (Ada, MI: Bethany House, 2008), 12-17.

22. *Evangelical Dictionary of Biblical Theology*, ed. Walter A. Elwell (Grand Rapids, MI: Baker Books, 1996), s.v. "Fatherhood of God," http://www.biblestudytools.com/dictionary/ fatherhood-of-god/.

23. Francis, *Evangelii Gaudium*, 3.

24. Charles de Foucauld qtd. in Ronda De Sola Chervin, *Quotable Saints* (Ann Arbor, MI: Servant Books, 1992), 199.

25. As noted in our book, *Sharing the Faith that You Love: Four Simple Ways to Be Part of the New Evangelization* (Frederick, MD: The Word Among Us Press, 2014), 45–48.

26. United States Conference of Catholic Bishops, *Go and Make Disciples: A National Plan and Strategy for Catholic Evangelization in the United States* (Washington, DC: USCCB Publishing, 2002), §12-14, http://www.usccb.org/beliefs-and-teachings/ how-we-teach/evangelization/go-and-make-disciples/what_is _evangelization_go_and_make_disciples.cfm.

27. Antonio Spadaro, SJ.

28. Immaculée Ilibagiza, *Left To Tell: Discovering God Amidst the Rwandan Holocaust* (Carlsbad, CA: Hay House, Inc., 2006).

29. Immaculée Ilibagiza, qtd. in Ernest Ogbozor, "Love and Forgiveness in Governance: Exemplars: Immaculée Ilibagiza," Beyond Intractibilty, http://www.beyondintractability.org/lfg/exemplars/ iilibagiza.

30. Damien de Veuster, SSCC, qtd. in "Brief Biography of St. Damien of Molokai," St. Damien of Molokai Catholic Church of Edmond, OK, http://www.stdamiens.org/02stdamienbiography.html.

31. For more about structured and spontaneous opportunities, read our book, *Sharing the Faith That You Love: Four Simple Ways to Be Part of the New Evangelization* (Frederick, MD: The Word Among Us Press, 2014).

32. John and Therese Boucher, "Am I a Leper?"Christkey, http://christkey.com/?page_id=105.

33. "Learn to Sing Dayenu," Great Jewish Music, http://www.great-jewishmusic.com/Midifiles/Passover/Dayenu.htm.

34. For more information on this inventory and the Called & Gifted™ Discernment Process, see the Catherine of Siena Institute's website, http://www.siena.org/Called-Gifted/called-a-gifted.

35. Agnes Sanford, *Sealed Orders, The Autobiography of a Christian Mystic* (Alucha, FL: Bridge-Logos Publishing, 1972).

36. St. John's parish bulletin, Oct 5, 2014. Used by permission. St. John's Church, Worcester, MA 01604.

37. Mother Teresa, *In the Heart of the World: Thoughts, Stories, and Prayers*, ed. Becky Benenate (San Francisco, CA: New World Library, 1997), 43.

38. C. S. Lewis, *Mere Christianity* (San Francisco, CA: HarperOne, 2009), 124.

39. Thomas Dubay, SM, 55.

40. Jeanne Kun, "Word Power: How to Make Your Speech a Blessing," *The Word Among Us,* http://wau.org/resources/article/re_word_power/.

41. Francis, Homily, February 16, 2014, http://m.vatican.va/content/francesco/en/homilies/2014/documents/papa-francesco_20140216_omelia-parrocchia-san-tommaso-apostolo.html.

42. Misty, "Come, Holy Spirit and Give Us Forbearance," Catholic Sistas: Perspective from the Neck, June 20, 2013, http://www.catholicsistas.com/2013/06/20/come-holy-spirit-and-give-us-forbearance/.

43. Christopher H. K. Persaud, *Famous People Speak about Jesus: A Compendium of Expressions of Praise and Reverence* (Bloomington, IN: Xlibris Publishing, 2004), 126.

44. For more about handling all the emotions involved in parenting young adults, see our book *Praying for Our Adult Sons and Daughters: Placing Them in the Heart of God* (Frederick, MD, The Word Among Us Press, 2012).

45. John XXIII, *Journal of a Soul: The Autobiography of Pope John XXIII* (New York City, NY: McGraw-Hill Book Co., 1965), 218.

46. Basilea Schlink, *Repentance: The Joy-Filled Life* (Grand Rapids, MI: Zondervan, 1968), 43.

47. Catherine of Siena, qtd. in Ronda De Sola Chervin, *Quotable Saints* (Ann Arbor, MI: Servant Books, 1992), 68.

48. John Gabriel Perboyre, qtd. in *PRAISE HIM! A Prayerbook for Today's Christian,* ed. by William Storey (Notre Dame, IN: Ave Maria Press, 1973), 83.

49. Leo Maasburg, *Mother Teresa of Calcutta: A Personal Portrait* (San Francisco, CA: Ignatius Press, 2011), 166–167.

50. Congregation for the Doctrine of the Faith. *Doctrinal Note on Some Aspects of Evangelization*, 4, http:// www.vatican.va/roman_curia/congregations/cfaith/documents/rc_con_cfaith_doc_20071203_nota-evangelizzazione_en.html.

51. *Go and Make Disciples,* 10.

52. Sherry Weddell, *Forming Intentional Disciples: The Path to Knowing and Following Jesus* (Huntington, IN: Our Sunday Visitor, 2012), 128-130.

53. Mother Teresa, 93-94.

54. Francis, *Evangelii Gaudium*, 24.

55. Augustine, "Prayer to the Holy Spirit," Catholic Doors Ministry, http://www.catholicdoors.com/prayers/english/p06900b.htm.

56. Paul VI,, *Gaudium et Spes* [Joy and Hope: The Pastoral Constitution on the Church in the Modern World], 1, http://www.vatican.va/archive/hist_councils/ii_vatican_council/documents/vat-ii_cons_19651207_gaudium-et-spes_en.html.

57. Francis, *Evangelii Gaudium,* 169.

58. Ibid., 172.

59. Adapted from "Come Holy Spirit," Catholic Online, http://www
    .catholic.org/prayers/prayer.php?p=331.

60. Francis, *Evangelii Gaudium*, 173.

61. Alfonso Capecelatro, *The Life of St. Philip Neri: Apostle of
    Rome*, Vol. 1 (London: Burns & Oats, 1984), 395.

62. Francis, *Evangelii Gaudium*, 273.

63. François Mauriac, qtd. in Fr. Thomas Rosica, CSB, "Faithful
    Stewards of God's Gifts and Mysteries: Biblical Reflection for
    25th Sunday in Ordinary Time," *ZENIT,* http://www.zenit.org/
    en/articles/faithful-stewards-of-god-s-gifts-and-mysteries.

Recommended Resources

Our websites, www.catholicevangelizer.com and www.johnandthereseboucher.com, provide resources for loving others as Jesus Christ does and for Catholic evangelization. Here are additional resources that you might find to be helpful.

Bennett, Art & Laraine. *The Emotions God Gave You: A Guide for Catholics to Healthy and Holy Living.* Frederick, MD: The Word Among Us Press, 2011.

Boucher, John & Therese. *Praying for Our Adult Sons and Daughters: Placing Them in the Heart of God.* Frederick, MD: The Word Among Us Press, 2012.

_____. *Sharing the Faith that You Love: Four Simple Ways to Be Part of the New Evangelization.* Frederick, MD: The Word Among Us Press, 2014.

Brown, Richard C. *When Ministry Is Messy: Practical Solutions to Difficult Problems.* Cincinnati, OH: Franciscan Media, 2006.

Dubay, Thomas, SM. *Caring: A Biblical Theology of Community.* Denville, NJ: Dimension Books, 1973.

_____. *Prayer Primer: Igniting a Fire Within.* Cincinnati, OH: Servant Books, 2002.

Francis. *Open Mind, Faithful Heart: Reflections on Following Jesus.* Edited by Gustavo Larrázabal. Translated by Joseph Owens, SJ. New York, NY: The Crossroads Publishing Company, 2013.

_____. *The Church of Mercy: A Vision for the Church.* Chicago, IL: Loyola Press, 2014.

_____. *The Joy of the Gospel: Evangelii Gaudium.* Washington, DC: USCCB Publishing, 2013.

Green, Thomas H., SJ. *Opening to God: A Guide to Prayer.* 2nd Edition. Notre Dame, IN: Sorin Books, 2006.

Gresham, John L., PhD. *Jesus 101: God and Man.* Liguori, MO: Liguori Publications, 2011.

Groeschel, Benedict J., CFR. *Stumbling Blocks or Stepping Stones: Spiritual Answers to Psychological Questions.* Mahwah, NJ: Paulist Press, 1987.

Hampsch, John H., CMF. *The Art of Loving God: Learning to Love and Follow Jesus in Daily Life.* Bloomington, IN: Xlibris Publishing, 2014.

Keating, Charles J. *Dealing with Difficult People: How You Can Come Out on Top in Personality Conflicts.* Mahwah, NJ: Paulist Press, 1984.

Keenan, James F., SJ. *The Works of Mercy: The Heart of Catholicism*. Lanham, MD: Rowman & Littlefield Publishers, Inc., 2007.

Kreeft, Peter. *Prayer for Beginners*. San Francisco, CA: Ignatius Press, 2000.

Lewis, C. S. *Surprised by Joy / The Four Loves*. Boston, MA: Houghton Mifflin Harcourt, 2011.

Linn, Dennis and Matthew Linn. *Healing Life's Hurts: Healing Memories through the Five Stages of Forgiveness*. Mahwah, NJ: Paulist Press, 1977.

Linn, Dennis, Sheila Fabricant Linn, and Matthew Linn. *Sleeping with Bread: Holding What Gives You Life*. Mahwah, NJ: Paulist Press, 1995.

MacNutt, Francis, PhD. *The Practice of Healing Prayer: A How-To Guide for Catholics*. Frederick, MD: The Word Among Us Press, 2010.

Martin, Ralph. *Hungry for God: Practical Help in Personal Prayer*. Cincinnati, OH: Servant Books, 2006.

Phelps, Owen, PhD. *The Catholic Vision for Leading Like Jesus: Introducing S³ Leadership—Servant, Steward, Shepherd*. Huntington, IN: Our Sunday Visitor, 2009.

Rinker, Rosalind. *Prayer: Conversing with God*. Grand Rapids, MI: Zondervan Publishing House, 1986.

Sofield, Loughlan, ST, Carroll Juliano, SHCJ, and Rosine Hammett, CSC. *Building Community: Christian, Caring, Vital*. Notre Dame, IN: Ave Maria Press, 1998.

Sofield, Loughlan, ST, Carroll Juliano, SHCJ, and Bishop Gregory M. Aymond. *Facing Forgiveness: A Catholic's Guide to Letting Go of Anger and Welcoming Reconciliation*. Notre Dame, IN: Ave Maria Press, 2007.

Thomas, Leo, OP, and Jan Alkire. *Healing as a Parish Ministry: Mending Body, Mind, and Spirit*. Notre Dame, IN: Ave Maria Press, 1992.

United States Conference of Catholic Bishops. *Go and Make Disciples: A National Plan and Strategy for Catholic Evangelization in the United States*. Washington, DC: USCCB Publishing, 2002.

Weddell, Sherry A. *Forming Intentional Disciples: The Path to Knowing and Loving Jesus*. Huntington, IN: Our Sunday Visitor, 2012.

Wuerl, Cardinal Donald. *The Light Is On for You: The Life-Changing Power of Confession*. Frederick, MD: The Word Among Us Press, 2014.

the WORD
among us®
The *Spirit* of Catholic Living

This book was published by The Word Among Us. Since 1981, The Word Among Us has been answering the call of the Second Vatican Council to help Catholic laypeople encounter Christ in the Scriptures.

The name of our company comes from the prologue to the Gospel of John and reflects the vision and purpose of all of our publications: to be an instrument of the Spirit, whose desire is to manifest Jesus' presence in and to the children of God. In this way, we hope to contribute to the Church's ongoing mission of proclaiming the gospel to the world so that all people would know the love and mercy of our Lord and grow ever more deeply in love with him.

Our monthly devotional magazine, *The Word Among Us*, features meditations on the daily and Sunday Mass readings, and currently reaches more than one million Catholics in North America and another half million Catholics in one hundred countries around the world. Our book division, The Word Among Us Press, publishes numerous books, Bible studies, and pamphlets that help Catholics grow in their faith.

To learn more about who we are and what we publish, log on to our website at www.wau.org. There you will find a variety of Catholic resources that will help you grow in your faith.

Embrace His Word, Listen to God . . .

www.wau.org